Brava!! Awesome!! Brave, Honest, Clear, Helpful, Connecting, Teaching, Learning, and Inspiring. You met your goals, Shirley. Your book is full of so many ideas, experiences, and feelings that your readers can take to their hearts and use to help them understand themselves more or understand someone who has suffered through abuse and its after effects.

I love and respect that you added the PTSD at the end. It's truthful. And it is part of your message—being deeply hurt and abused as a child doesn't just disappear because of age or accomplishment. There is hope, healing, and a community of souls who support, share, and assist one another. We both belong to that community.

I also like the feeling that you, as author, are genuinely sharing your life with me as a reader. It makes the reading flow, even the very sad parts. There is so much I like about your book—your poetry, your letters... and more.

I feel so happy and proud of you, of your writing, of all that you have done with your life—of the tenderness you show your inner child; of the care you show others, your family, and many others.

You wrote with great respect about your children as children and as adults now. You didn't expose them—what I mean is that you didn't put them in a position as far as I can see that would put them in a spotlight and feel a need to answer to anyone who might be intrusive. You owned your own material. It is beautiful.

It was wonderful to read about Ken and the wonderful life partner he is.

Thank you for sharing your "work" with me.

Love,

Bonnie Garner Lockwood, MA, NCPsyA

T0149887

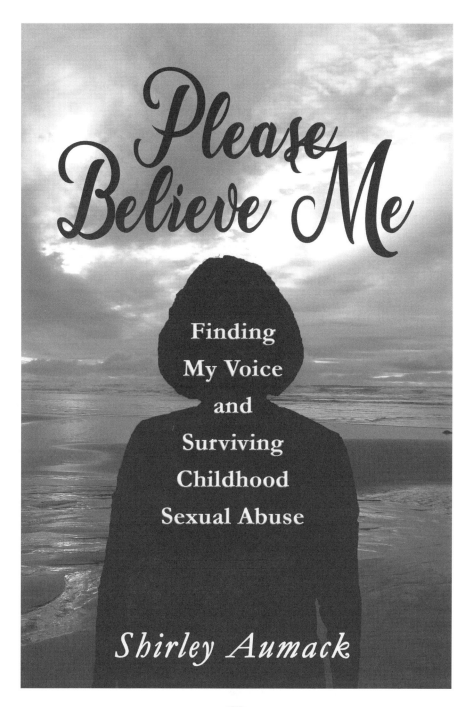

Please Believe Me

Finding
My Voice
and
Surviving
Childhood
Sexual Abuse

Shirley Aumack

Robert D. Reed Publishers

Robert D. Reed Publishers • Bandon, OR

Robert D. Reed Publishers
P.O. Box 1992
Bandon, OR 97411
Phone: 541-347-9882; Fax: -9883
E-mail: 4bobreed@msn.com
Website: www.rdrpublishers.com

Editor: Cleone Lyvonne Reed
Designer: Amy Cole
Cover: Cleone Lyvonne Reed

Soft Cover ISBN: 978-1-944297-62-6
EBook ISBN: 978-1-944297-63-3

Library of Congress Control Number: 2020936911

Designed and Formatted in the United States of America

Dedications

My grandmother: the one adult in my life who loved me in the purist and best way, who comforted me and stood by me and with me through all of my trials. I could always count on you although I never told you.

My husband: who truly meant his wedding vows and who, through all of my trials, was always steadfastly by my side, never once failing me in my time of need.

I also want to recognize my brother who was there for me during my childhood each and every day. I love you so much for your constant support while we were immersed in my nightmare.

I want to thank my boys who grew up to be the fine men I hoped for and who make me proud every day.

And to all those who have come before me and will come after me, I wish that you will find love and help in your journey to survival. Please never give up hope as there is always a new day that can bring peace from the raging storm.

And to those who are helping and loving us survivors, may your understanding grow and blossom in the light of my story.

Acknowledgments

Someone once said that you need only one person in your life to love you with no reservations and you can be a success. In my life I was lucky to have two such people in my life, and I am eternally grateful to both of them each and every day.

My grandmother at age 97

My grandmother was the first person in my life and the one adult in my childhood life who loved me in the purist and best way, who comforted me and stood by me and with me through all of my trials. I could always count on her although I never told her about what had happened to me with my father. She was with me for a very long time since she lived to be 100 years old and died when I was 42 years old. Her remarkable life showed me that I could overcome any adversity that life threw my way and still be upright at the end of the day. She was a fighter! I still think about her every day and have memories of her all over our house including her jewelry which I still wear very often. My newest tribute to her is framed with her photographs from when she was in her 20's, cards for her birthdays from Jimmy Carter, Ronald Reagan, and George Bush as well as three sashes from the German ship she sailed on in 1894 on her journey from Germany with her mother and brother.

Sometimes you meet someone who will change your life in a very profound way. For me, this was Eleanor O'Sullivan. Eleanor was a client of mine for several years. She was the movie reviewer for our regional newspaper, the Asbury Park Press, and she wrote many other articles and features for the paper as well. In addition, she also writes articles for Financial Advisor Magazine. At one of our visits together I mentioned to her that I was writing a book and she volunteered to help me. She became my go-to person and the first person who read my book as I wrote it chapter by chapter. I can honestly say there would be no book without her. Her editing skills were invaluable to me! Her encouragement during my rough times was a great gift that I needed many times during this journey. So, if this book moves you in any way, you can not only credit me but also her. Thank you Eleanor!

My husband is the second wonderful gift God gave me in my life. At our 25th Anniversary party as we were all laughing and having fun, someone asked us the secret of a long marriage. You answered without a moment's hesitation: "Some people say that marriage is a 50/50 proposition but that is not true. Sometimes you have to give 100% and get nothing in return. And sometimes you need 100% but have nothing to give." Everyone sat in stunned silence including me!

You truly have been my rock since I met you when I was fourteen years old. I remember what I was like then… I hated my parents and was just living there until I could leave. When you came into my life

I knew I had found someone so different from me. I was very serious about everything... politics, war, caring for others and not letting them be hurt, and trying to see that people have what they need in life. I was not interested in ridiculous news and TV shows and movies that showed no social relevance. You were so very lighthearted and happy and definitely had nothing heavy on your heart. You were the example of someone who did not have a perfect life (whatever that would look like) but were so contented with your life. You were and are a rock to me every day of our life. And you are just so much fun! You filled our lives with so much laughter and still do. You can laugh and make a joke about just about anything.

I remember with tears how difficult life was for you during my painful discovery of my childhood. You were profoundly affected by these revelations but stood by me and held me every time I needed you. No matter what, you were there. I remember how you acted then. On a typical Saturday morning you got up in the morning and left me in stunned silence in bed knowing that I would probably be there all day. You took care of the boys and kept yourself busy all day while I laid in bed unable to move, suffering from devastating depression and horrifying memories of my childhood. During all of this you never said an unkind word to me. You took care of the boys and me. You loved me and showed it by your words and your actions. And you told me you loved me as many times as I needed to hear it. You came into our room looking very serious but always gave me a big smile, your face lighting up our room with light and life. You never once disappointed me.

And now, as we grow old together and I start on another amazing journey in our lives, you stand by me and with me every minute of every day. And you will continue to be with me for many years to come if God so deems it to be...

There truly are no words to describe how wonderful our life together has been. It's been quite a ride. A beautiful life, each day, no matter what, secure and blessed by our love for each other. Thank you for choosing me, marrying me, taking care of me, and being there to let me love you!

Therapist Acknowledgements

My first therapist was someone who came into my life through someone I admired and trusted. I was doing well but had a great deal of anxiety and finally wanted to try something I knew very little about but decided to try. His name was Steve. It was many years ago and I have not been able to find him although I would have liked him to write something about me in those early years from his perspective. I do want to thank him for his hard work and commitment to me through my early trials to find peace in my life. I remember him telling me once that a good therapist can really tell what the new person is seeking to find out or correct in their lives and how serious it is on the first visit. He knew after that visit that I had something very serious on my heart and that it would take quite a long time to dig through the layers and get to the truth. And so it began. I want to acknowledge his hard work, discipline, and serious, and I mean serious, dedication to helping me. It worked and I began to heal, slowly and so painfully, and he recommended that I go on to a therapist that had a group of sexual abuse survivors that she worked with and he felt it would be good for me.

And so Bonnie Garner Lockwood, MA, NCPsyA came into my life. The group was painfully uncomfortable for me. I never thought about others that were in the same place that I was in. In truth, I never wanted to hear their stories. I never wanted to cry about their terrors. But Bonnie, with her amazingly soothing voice and her beautiful and knowing spirit and experience, was able to come up with activities in which we could all participate; it was incredible. I began to use Bonnie as my personal therapist. She was so helpful in getting me to feel so much more comfortable in my skin. I left her after she had taught me so many ways to handle every-day life. Thank God for her in my life.

After I had written the book and was in the middle of it all, I began to suffer again. It was truly awful. My psychiatrist was very worried about me and recommended I enter Partial Hospitalization Program to help me through my PTSD (Post Traumatic Stress Syndrome). It was an all-day program, but I was able to go home each evening because my husband drove me each way to the program. After the program I was told I had to have a trauma specialist to continue to help me with the program that I had been attending. The program found one for me and I began to see Denise Murdock, LCSW.

Denise was very different from my other two therapists because she was all about practical ways to learn how to understand my reactions to my surroundings and thoughts and how to deal with all of it. Denise is still in my life whenever I need her and she means the world me. Thank you so much for being in my life.

And I just want to say that no matter how dark life seems in the moment (and it will happen from time to time), just remember to reach out and find that someone who will help you when you need it. Please, never give up or give in.

Contents

Foreword

Shirley Aumack is an amazing woman. She has lived a life of light and love. She married well, truly finding a partner who worked with her to build a business and a home. Together they raised two boys who adore her and her husband. Young men who keep in touch and come home often and who are themselves healthy and good men.

What you would never guess from looking at Shirley and her current life is her back story. She was sexually abused as a young girl by her father and then he piled on the emotional abuse. He told her she was unlovable and deserved what she got. "No one will ever love you." He only stopped because she reached an age where she feared he would get her pregnant and someone would know.

The authorities declined to believe her when she told them. Only her brother knew the truth and he let her hide in his room at night when he could. He tried as a teenager to make his father leave her alone. Shirley was very aware that he was scarred by this.

Like many survivors of abuse, Shirley's history was offset by her sharp mind as well as a great partner who allowed her to move forward despite the abuse. Still, life is not perfect. She continues to this day to struggle with doubt, and at times self-loathing. The abuse has colored relationships and she struggles at times to sort out her own distortions, from what people really mean when they say things to her. There are uncomfortable moments when she is reminded of her past, sometimes by very innocent actions of others or just by someone's presence.

She has had to learn that an abusive parent will lie to you as well as to the world and not everything she was told is true. She was, and is, loved by many. She is valuable to her husband and her children. She has been a blessing to many friends and family, as well as to strangers who she sees need something. She is a good person, and that has nothing to do with how her father violated her trust and her body.

Shirley has a light to show the way through the dark world often inhabited by survivors of Child Sexual Abuse. She has been there and come out on the other side, bruised but not beaten, and ready to share that this is not then and that, with help, it is possible to not only survive but to thrive, as she has done.

Bravo Shirley, for writing the book, and for continuing the push to get it published for the greater good!

—Denise Murdock, LCSW, Therapist

Introduction

When Shirley Aumack, the author, begged her dad to stop sexually abusing her, he responded:

> "No one cares what I do to you.
> I don't love you,
> No one loves you,
> And no one will EVER love you."

How does a little girl, or anyone, ever heal from such a horrific message? It seems inhumane, unbelievable, atrocious, mean, sadistic, cruel, callous, barbarous, perverted, vicious, savage, brutal, the list goes on! The message was extremely devastating, as were his actions of raping her starting when she was just eight years old. Compounding the pain was having a mother who was emotionally vacant.

Like many people who are severely abused, Shirley overcompensated her feelings of low self-worth by excelling at everything she did—academically, professionally, and personally as a wife, mother, friend, and retired woman.

Shirley has raised two wonderful sons, enjoys two grandchildren, has maintained a healthy and loving marriage, made countless friends, and created lasting relationships with clients in a several-decades-long career. Her love has poured out of her, and this love has been reciprocated multi-fold.

Shirley writes to help survivors understand themselves better and to help "non-survivors" understand the anguish and agony that haunts those who have been sexually (and emotionally) abused. She succeeds in both goals. She wants anyone who has been abused to gain strength to carry on after reading about her triumphs in living a loving life in spite of (and perhaps because of) her horrendous abusive experiences.

Even though Shirley's life and mine have several parallels, her words rang loudly in my mind when I awoke this morning. That is what a good book should do... make a person reflect on his or her own life and become more understanding and compassionate of other people's lives. She writes beautifully. Her prose reads like poetry.

Shirley is a gifted storyteller making the book a quick read. But her messages will stay with me for a very long time. She covers unflinchingly details of her life including her despair and devastation. But her book is one not only of surviving but also of thriving. In addition to horrifying images, she includes laugh-out-loud stories.

Ultimately this book is inspiring and empowering, hopeful and healing. Shirley's life serves as a testament to the preciousness of all life, the transformative power of love, the triumph of the human spirit, and the need for humor. Her life is summed up well by her t-shirt in the "About the Author" section: "I survived the 60's twice!"

—Lois Einhorn, Ph.D.,
Professor at Binghamton University in New York,
Author *of Forgiveness and Child Abuse: Would YOU Forgive?*
Compassionate Fairy Tales and *Why Do We All Love Dr. Seuss?*

Preface

I am a survivor of childhood sexual abuse at the hand of my father. This book takes you on my journey out of the hell that I endured as a child to a productive and almost wonderful life. I hope my book will help survivors to understand themselves better. And I also hope it will help non-survivors to understand the heartache and devastation that haunts sexual abuse victims and survivors.

During my struggle to have control over my life, I used the lessons I learned from my pain and sorrow as a tool to help others with the troubling issues in their lives. I could never fight for myself at all after being crippled by the abuse but I was and am a fighter, so I was able to fight like hell for others in their times of need. I derived great peace from helping others and knowing that some who I had helped out there in the world would hopefully then help others, creating a continuum of support and understanding. There is a very long list of people who have said to me, "How can I ever repay you for what you have done for me?" And each and every time I have told them not to worry for when I need help, someone will be there for me.

I had a father who was a horrible human being and a mother who was dead inside. They were both cruel to me and never stepped up to the plate to help me when I needed it. I was eight years old when the sexual abuse started and it continued until I was eleven. The effects continue to this day and will for the rest of my life.

But I am a survivor which means that I have broken the chains that my parents wrapped around me. It is often said that a person needs only one person to believe in them and to love them in order to be a successful human being and to be successful in their lives. I was and am very lucky and blessed to have had two of those people in my life. The first one was my maternal grandmother and the second one is my husband of 50 years. They made me feel important, loved, and valued and gave me the freedom to be myself. They also loved me so much that I almost could always feel grateful to be alive and to be me. Because of them I was able to try to help others by listening very carefully to hear what is in people's hearts and minds and not just what comes out of their mouths. What people say and how they say it is a window into their souls. Whether you agree or disagree with them is not as important as understanding what drives their opinions and their choices in life.

No matter who or what has hurt you, you can survive. Survival is the first step, but the ultimate goal is to have a life that is meaningful and happy. In other words, to thrive. Always remember that no matter how hopeless your situation seems to be, you should never give up or give in. Even if you cannot help yourself you can find help and you can help someone else and you can prevail in making a difference in the world. Helping others will give you hope, great joy, and peace. In my childhood I longed to find this one person, a teacher, a minister, a parent who would be there for me and who I could tell what had transpired in my life, but it never happened. There were many times when it seemed I had no reason to hope.

You can never forget what happened in your past, but you can come to recognize the pain when it returns and learn how to deal with it. You may not always be successful. As you try you will become stronger and better at being able to overcome your past. You will never know when the past will come back to haunt you. For example, one Christmas I received a very inexpensive gift from someone close to me. It may seem strange to those of you who have not suffered as I did, but it upset me to the degree that I almost immediately felt that I was not valued and I sincerely and immediately wanted to commit suicide. It haunted me for days that the other party felt that I was so

6

unworthy. With the help of my loving family, I was able to get past this and realize that these feelings were coming from the past. These experiences are deeply troubling, but you can learn ways to attempt to handle the pain no matter how close the abuser is to you or how deep the pain is. That is your goal.

I believe this book needed to be written. It needs to help those who are still grieving and weeping over their sexual abuse. The book also aims to help the rest of society who truly need to grasp the consequences of the abuse. When we hear about or from someone who has been sexually abused or harassed, we generally listen intently as they describe their experience(s). However, people who have never had this experience do not think about the long-term ramifications of the abuse. People do not understand that the experience does not just disappear; it lasts forever. It shakes confidence and it can ruin the life of the abused and can change the abused in ways the non-abused find difficult to understand and appreciate. It makes the abused feel filthy and disgusting. As a victim of sexual abuse you will typically feel that there is something wrong **with** you rather than questioning the wrong that has been done **to** you. That is because of the secrecy and the entrapment of the relationship and the ability of the abuser to use a great deal of his own energy to manipulate the abused.

Those who have never been abused also need to understand that the abuse is not about sex but about power. It is now time for everyone to understand the power of sexual abuse and harassment and how it changes a person in so many ways. You will understand this important message after you read this book.

It will help all members of society to understand how sexual harassment and abuse hurts anyone who has endured it. It will help people who have a friend or acquaintance who needs help and love. It will help medical personnel and therapists and people of all types such as teachers and parents and spouses and anyone who ministers to others to better help the wounded. For example, I always tell my doctors about the abuse so I get the most careful care from them, and they always explain to me each and everything they will do if touching me. It really helps me feel more comfortable when I visit a physician.

It will help people to understand the power of love and the power of the Lord and how both are real and tangible. It will also help me to begin a new chapter in my life of helping people in a much broader and more powerful way.

I have triumphed and I am free. I thank God every day for His love, guidance, and the prayerful retreat He provides and for the wonderful people he has placed in my life. In addition, I have to thank all of the people who allowed me to make a difference in their lives. Without all of you I would not be in the wonderful place where I am today.

one

My Life Changed Forever

*I*ncest began for me at the age of eight years old. I was a very strong, intelligent, hard-headed little girl with bright red curls and a free spirit that was palpable. In spite of my childhood sexual abuse, that spirit lives on today. This is my story of survival and how I learned to cope with my past and have a wonderful life.

My life changed forever the day my eight-year-old self was home alone with my father and I decided to confront him and quietly ask him to stop the bad things he was doing to me. He was sitting behind his desk as I asked him to stop. His face blazed red as he slowly and quietly stood up and slammed his hand on the desk, leaned over and, with his anger dripping from his mouth and covering me, said to me, "No one cares what I do to you. I don't love you, no one loves you, and no one will EVER love you."

These words and the horrid ramifications of his actions and his words have been with me ever since.

One of my earliest memories of my childhood was a day at the beach when I was three years old. I was playing at the water's edge and all of a sudden a wave took me out to sea.

As I was being carried out by the waves, I could feel myself float-ing and twisting and swirling away in the surf. It was a beautiful, clear, warm summer day with the sunbeams dancing on the waves and the vastness of the ocean all around me. I felt like I was floating peacefully in the waves with a warm breeze caressing me. I remember seeing my father's shoes under the water and thinking, "What is he doing in the water with his moccasins on?"

Years later I wrote an essay about this experience and how I asked my father, "Why did you save me? You should have let me die at your hand by letting me drown rather than to try to murder me by inches, slowly, painfully…a death that would be so excruciatingly slow that it would still be happening 40 years after you saved me from the sea.

"Try to imagine what it has been like for me in the dark moments of discovery so many years after the sexual abuse actually happened… the long and dreadfully difficult minutes, hours, days, and weeks that it took me to fully understand and remember what my father had done to me as a child. Try to imagine all that you know about the ocean and its beauty and peace and warmth paralleled by its violence and cold and fury during a storm. All of the images, thoughts, and feelings of the ocean coming together all at once. Try to imagine the overwhelming pain, the disturbing truths of discovery all crashing down on me with the power and fury of the raging surf and the ach-ing, searing, and desperate thoughts and feelings of being betrayed and the despondent feelings of guilt and shame that made me fer-vently desire to kill myself.

"At the same time, try to imagine the experience of letting others take care of me, love me, hold me, hug me, cry with me, reassure me for the very first time in my life, coupled with the experience of trust-ing, knowing that there truly are people here to protect me, people who will listen to my silent cries for help and will help me overcome my terror of being abandoned as I was as a child, friends and family who will not let me slip into the deep, dark abyss, paralyzed by the fear, the filth, the horror and the terror of what I had lived through as a child.

"I will survive in a true rebirth of my human spirit, reborn out of the terror of what has come before. But, it is over. It can't touch me in that way again; my triumph of the human spirit proves that there is always hope. And someday, I will truly know that safety is at the core of my existence and peace is in my grasp."

I wrote this in April of 1992.

I hope that all who have come before me and those who come after will see from my story that hope is a powerful weapon against cruelty. The life that I have led and the peace that I have found, in spite of everything, and my desire to share my story with all of you should stand as a single testament to the human spirit. I believe that there is an unknowable number who, like me, have suffered and also gone on to have meaningful lives in spite of the horrific difficulty they have withstood.

two

My Family Tree

My father was born in 1911 the oldest child of five children. There were Herbert, Helen, Wilmot, Alice, and Ray. My father was the quiet, uptight man who felt so small, so unimportant and unheard. However, the people in the family described him as "always a gentleman." They did not see that he was depressed and seething with anger and feelings of being dismissed and never taken seriously. He was very intelligent but constricted intellectually and constantly being ridiculed for his overzealous thought patterns and processes that took everything to the umpteenth level of study and contemplation before he made even the simplest decisions. His thinking was like a Rube Goldberg illustration being created. An example of this would be illustrated by how he would tie the knots on our sailboat and trailer to see that it was properly fastened together for the Saturday ride to the lake. It always took him several hours to do. It was painful for my brother and me to watch him. When we finally got to the lake, many of the other boaters were coming into the shore to get ready for their trips back home. Oftentimes they would comment on the crazy ropes, loops, ties, and knots used to secure our boat.

My father felt he had no power in his life and this caused seething anger. He was very aloof and distant. An innocent child with no voice, I fit the bill as the perfect victim of his need to be in control. He needed to have something to control since he did not have any control in the rest of his life.

His politics were not Democratic or Republican or Conservative or Liberal. He was a true Reactionary, a word that is not often heard today. A reactionary is someone who is opposed to progressive social or political change and who wants to return to the status quo of the past. He studied economics at the Henry George School. Henry George was an economist and a social philosopher. At the school of economics students were taught using reactionary principles.

"As Henry George witnessed the growth of modern civilization he was profoundly disturbed by the trends toward centralized control, Gargantuan taxation, disregard for the rights of person and property which he saw setting in, and, which carried far enough, he believed, must bring social progress to a halt. He found answers in measures of greater freedom rather than less freedom. He identified freedom of opportunity as the natural remedy for current problems."

—These are some of the comments about
Henry George written by John Lawrence Monroe,
director of the Chicago Henry George School, 1935 – 1968.

My father was a very odd bird. Those who knew him best said so, even people whom I spoke to about him after his death. He was very quiet, very serious, and a true intellectual. He never felt that he had any power in his life. I never remember signs of affection. I do not remember him hugging me, holding, me, kissing me, or telling me that he loved me.

When he came home from work, like a robot, he immediately went upstairs to his room and came down when he had changed his clothes and fastidiously put away his suit and tie and shoes in the closest. I never saw a piece of his clothing thrown casually on the floor or on a chair. When he came downstairs, he sat in his favorite chair in the

14

living room, never asking anyone about their day or telling us about his. He then read his newspaper. Once in a while, in a bid for attention, I would stick my head under the newspaper page and say "Boo" and smile and laugh. That did not go over well with him. My brother Richard was treated in the same way, with no affection or interest. Unlike me, Richard was a quiet child with a docile personality. He did not provoke our father. I, on the other hand, provoked my father at every opportunity in my bid for childish attention.

Another odd or abnormal habit that my father had was to make notes about how he was treated and mistreated by the great Prudential Insurance Company in Newark, New Jersey, where he worked for 40 years. Thousands of little white scraps of papers discussing his issues of that day were kept in the top drawer of his chest. I imagined they were still there, kept by my mother, even though he had been dead for many years. I am grateful that I found a few to share.

The Prudential kept him on as that is what they did in those days. In the past companies would not be as quick to fire workers who were not performing as they should in their present position and try to move them to other positions which hopefully would suit them better. He also had two brothers and a brother-in-law working there, which probably helped his retention. But he was downgraded consistently until he had the grand position of reading mail that mail sorters could not determine to which department the particular letter should be directed so the letter could be answered by the proper party. It was a very menial job. He used to say that he was going to write a book about the way he was mistreated. Here are samples of a few notes that I found written by him in his original phrasing:

1. Some have been taught, or have somehow come to the conclusion, that they are not to think but merely accept what others tell them. This type of behavior is flattery to self- appointed "superiors", but the danger is in the fact that the same sort of thing kept the dark ages dark. We could lose this country if most of the people took it for granted

they know very little, and that everyone else is an expert in something, thereby letting control of the country go to any opportunists. (1956)

2. I suspect that he (my father's boss) treated, or practiced on, others with the same tactics. The objective was probably to "prepare" the person for the loss of reputation and job standing by making worker think he was worthless and anyone else would be on KCA's (the boss) side in the event of any test of ability of the employee. (And subsequent management will ignore good work by person knocked down, for convenience and to avoid contesting record). (1959)

I also found a note from when he was an older man suffering from Parkinson's disease. I believe he had to retire disabled in 1970. This note is dated 6/9/1972 and signed by him.

"If there should be anything mysterious about my death or if it should be sudden, have autopsy performed. On Nov. 30, 1972, Jan. 3, 1972, and April 3, 1972, two attempts were made each time to take blood samples. Dark-haired nurse 1st (left arm), Dr. Cuccia 2nd, & Mrs. Nilson 3rd. Last two probed around much more than necessary and last one on the first try mentioned a 'serum' (Warning?). My arm (R. last two times) was black and blue several days after probing. Probes were into my elbow joints. After 4/3/72 visit to Dr. my face and fingers were pink like my father's when he had a stroke."

You can see what I mean about his paranoid tendencies.

His parents' backgrounds were very different than the norm. My orphaned paternal grandmother grew up in an orphanage. She had the bearing and personality of someone who had been raised in an institutional setting. She was very rigid, uptight, and cross. She did not like any of the spouses who her children chose and she was controlling. I remember many occasions when she was angry with her grandchildren. There was one time when I was seven or eight years old when she came to visit us and she saw that I had on nail polish. Our neighbor had polished my nails and I was so pleased about it as it was the first time I had polished nails. I came happily home running to show my mother laughing all the way. My grandmother was outside sitting in the backyard, and she was horrified by my nails. She very nastily berated my mother and me about how inappropriate it was at my age. She certainly never enjoyed any of us. Like my father, it was unusual for her to smile or respond to humor.

My grandfather was left with a maiden aunt as a young boy while his parents and his older sibling resettled in the West. They never came back for him or sent for him. The maiden aunt was a very strange person who dressed him up in a Little Lord Fauntleroy outfit and made him sit in the front window like a mannequin so he could be seen by the townspeople as they strolled by. He was not allowed to play with other children. In spite of his abandonment and strange lifestyle, he had a wonderful, warm personality. I remember him dearly as a happy and loving human being. Unfortunately he died when I was 3.

I have been told by my cousin and my mother that the three oldest siblings lived with their wealthy maiden aunt each summer for years when they were children. We have often wondered what happened to them while they were there. It seems so odd that all three had personality disorders, while the younger two, who did not spend summers with the aunt, seemed to be mostly well adjusted. But of course we do know that each was deeply affected by something that the younger ones appeared not to have suffered. This difference was revealed in the personality disorders the older three siblings exhibited.

Helen, the second child, exhibited the qualities of a person who today would be labeled as obsessive compulsive. Her home was polished clean to the nines and everything had to be perfect. There was never even one item out of place. When we visited our Aunt Helen, she would wait outside the bathroom when anyone was using it. After the person exited that bathroom, she would rush in and check things over and at the very least she would dry out the sink after you washed your hands. We were kids at the time, and the song, "Does Your Chewing Gum Lose Its Flavor on the Bedpost Overnight" was popular. My brother and I and our cousins contemplated what she would do if we tried putting our gum on the bedpost. But making a very intelligent decision, we did not test our theory, although I certainly wanted to do it. Her daughter, my cousin, and the oldest of the cousins was never allowed to have friends over to her house and she was always in trouble with her parents. She married very young and was always in abusive relationships and was an alcoholic. Her brother Edward, the compliant one, went along with his parents in order to keep the peace. He was killed in a car accident going back to college after Thanksgiving break. At the time, my cousin's parents told her that her brother was decapitated and that they wished she was the one who had died. He was not decapitated but she believed that for many years. My Uncle Ray, who lived in New Hampshire where the accident had occurred and who identified the body, emphatically denied that he was decapitated and told my cousin that. He was shocked that her parents had told her that but I don't believe anyone in the family was all that surprised since the parents idolized their son, Edward, and did not think much about their daughter.

Wilmot, the third child, was overwhelmed with and overcome by anger. My cousins tell me that he was always angry about something. My older cousin in Wilmot's family was the one who pushed him to his limit and who did not want to give in to his anger. She stood up to her father. She would not acquiesce to Wilmot's demands and my uncle used become so enraged that he would even chase her around the yard when my cousin went outside to escape his anger. Wilmot's anger was always simmering under the surface, and once it started it would just get worse and worse as he could not make it stop. And to make it worse for him he was married to a Southern gal who spoke and acted slowly, which must not have helped. My uncle was hospitalized three times for depression and anxiety (a nervous breakdown). My father developed Parkinson's disease when he was in his 50's. He walked very slowly and haltingly. He and my mother were visiting Wilmot on Lake Winnipesaukee in New Hampshire where Wilmot and Pat had retired. Wilmot wanted to take my father out on his boat but my father was walking too slowly for Wilmot. What do you think Wilmot did? Without a word he wrapped his arms around my father from the back and picked up my father and carried him to the edge of the dock and threw his legs over the side of the boat. My father was not hurt and off the four of them went for the boat ride.

Alice, the fourth child, was the most normal of the children. I absolutely loved her. I had her spirit of fun and laughter and we often had a laugh together. She used to sing a wonderful song:

"Alice, where are you going? Upstairs to take a bath. Alice, with legs like toothpicks and a neck like a giraffe. Alice, fill up and bathtub, pull out the plug and then, Holy Moses, bless my soul, there goes Alice down the hole! Blub, blub, blub!!"

I could never bring myself to tell her that my father, her brother, was abusing me sexually, or that my mother had done nothing to help me or to stop the abuse. I feared that Aunt Alice would not believe me and it would mean the end of our sweet and loving relationship.

Ray, the youngest child, was my other favorite and he was crazy about me. He could always make me smile, and he listened to me and we could discuss almost everything. I cannot say that he was the calmest person but he was certainly better than the others. At least I think so. He seemed to make more rational decisions about his life and did not seem as angry or controlling. He moved to New Hampshire after his four children were born to pursue his own business. He started out with a home and 40 acres on Suncook Lake. The property had three cabins on it which the family rented out in the summer. He also had a full-time job at that time. We had many wonderful times there enjoying the lake and being together. As young cousins we always enjoyed our times together and this was just another time during our childhoods when we could be in a wonderful place and be together.

After many years at the lake Uncle Ray moved to Concord and then to Lincoln New Hampshire where he had a general store. It also had a breakfast and lunch counter, a Laundromat, and arcade games. After that he moved to Buena Vista, Virginia, and had a furniture and appliance store. He did like to be in control and I don't think he ever reached the level of success that he wanted. The boys worked with him but I imagine that was tough for them. He was controlling, to say the least, and I don't think he took anyone else's feelings into account as he changed jobs and moved the family from place to place.

My mother's family was totally and completely different from my father's family. First of all my mother was an only child. My grandmother had a terrible delivery and the doctor took forceps and ripped her open so that the baby could navigate the birth canal. That damage was the end of my grandmother's childbearing.

As I said earlier in the Preface, a person needs only one person in their life to believe in them for the person to be a success and able to overcome terrible tragedies. For me, this was not my mother.

My mother was a weak person. She was very bright and even skipped a grade in high school. But she was clueless about many things. She performed all the basic parental duties: She cooked for us and bathed us, cleaned the house, helped us to get off to school, and she took us to the doctor and to our activities and welcomed our friends to our house. All of our basic wants were covered. But our emotional needs were never, ever, not even once, discussed, handled, or tenderly cared for and our souls were left wanting: we were never loved, hugged, or kissed. We grew up in a home that was devoid of any positive emotion.

As I said my mother was dead inside. She never faced any of her problems head-on but just wished they would go away. As a mother this made her very unsupportive. She was unable to face our childhood issues such as my brother's shyness as we grew up, and we were on our own when it came to confronting the world. In our family, there was no kissing or hugging or saying "I love you." She cared for us but not about us. My father made a wise choice when he married her. She was just clueless about life and how to handle it. My father had very poor coping skills but she had none. If a problem came up she would just say "think happy thoughts." It was like an anthem to her.

My father hated everyone because they were always wrong and he was always right. He complained to my mother constantly about the people in his life who he had contact with, whether they were people at work, his family, and the people from the church. He was always angry with people but could never confront anyone or discuss any of his issues with the people in his life. He just let his disagreements fester. My mother was incapable of handling any emotional situations and devoid of any ideas as to what would be an answer to any problems that came up. She became hysterical if you brought a problem to her.

Here is a perfect example of what I mean. I started taking piano lessons when I was in the fifth grade. My brother had taken them before me. I loved listening to him play and watching him, partly because our parakeet, Lucky, used to perch on the top of the music and sing and nibble on the music book. At some point, Richard just grew tired of playing and stopped his lessons. I loved playing the piano and enjoyed my teacher. I practiced frequently and improved with time. My teacher was very encouraging. When I was in the seventh grade our town decided to have a talent show for youngsters and I signed up to audition. After all of these years I even remember the piece. It was "Fur Elise" by Ludwig von Beethoven. At the audition there was a microphone on the piano and the sound was distorted so I became disoriented and upset. When I went home and told my mother what happened she immediately became hysterical and was holding her face crying out "Oh no, not you too; oh, this is so awful. Oh how I wish this hadn't happened. Oh, I don't know what to say." How does a twelve-year- old respond to that? I couldn't ask any questions because she was already out of control. I could only imagine what she would do if I had questioned her.

In the end, as luck would have it, the judges liked me and asked me to be the master of ceremonies for the show and to introduce all of the acts in my own special style. I had a wonderful time and enjoyed the laughter and the lightness of what I did that night. I was relaxed and comfortable, and many people complimented me about how I was an act all by myself and how I added to the show. I remember I was very animated and enthusiastic about how I introduced each act. Unfortunately, however, this incident caused me to lose heart in playing the piano and I stopped practicing. Soon after that the piano teacher told my mother that since I had lost interest there was no reason for me to continue the lessons. This was such a shame because all of my life I have loved music and it has meant so much to me and brought me great joy. Of course my parents never questioned me for giving up. It was another difficult time in my life where I never received proper parental support.

My maternal grandmother and her brother Herbert were brought to the United States from Bremen, Germany, in 1894. My great grandmother was a widow when they arrived in New York City. She soon found a new husband who happened to be a chef at the Waldorf-Astoria. I remember the stories of how they ate the food he brought home, especially steak and eggs for breakfast. I think that was her favorite. My great-grandmother had a child with her new husband. His name was Eugene, and the fact that he was not one of the original two children was hidden from the other children until they were probably in their fifties. In fact I have recently found family papers that show that the two children who were not born of this marriage were told that Karl was their father as well. Secrets were kept in those days, and it is certainly amazing that the older children had no idea that they had a different father. At that time they lived in Harlem in New York, which is where many of the German immigrants new to this country settled. My great-grandmother's second husband died young in his 30's, so my mother never knew him. Oh, the stories that my grandmother told me. They had no electricity, only gas lamps, and they had an icebox where food was kept cold by putting a big hunk of ice in the box. I remember the story of how she had her tonsils out at the doctor's office and then took the trolley home with her mother.

My grandmother, as she grew older, was my great-grandmother's servant. My great-grandmother was a very strong-willed, haughty, self-absorbed woman. She made many German friends who were quite wealthy, so, even though she was poor she lived within the world of the rich and she even inherited money and jewelry and art from her friends, which my brother and I still have today. But being a widow she did not have an easy time living daily life due to financial constraints. The reason this is important to this story is because she kept my grandmother as her servant, as I said before. My grandmother did all of the daily work around the house. My grandmother was also unusual because in approximately 1910 she was a working woman, who worked for the Pennsylvania Railroad as a secretary. I am sure she used most of this money for her mother's support.

My grandmother was discouraged from meeting men and thinking of her own life as a wife and possibly a mother. Amazingly independent and desiring her own life, she met a man on the train commuting to work. They fell in love on the train and they never really dated besides these meetings. Because my grandmother was wise in her understanding of her mother's personality and her powerful bitter tongue, my grandmother and grandfather eloped and then told my great-grandmother. I can only imagine the vitriol this caused. My grandmother told me about it many times, but I am convinced that I cannot even begin to imagine what that meeting was like. And my grandfather…he was the gentlest soul I have ever had the pleasure of knowing. He was a beautiful, peaceful man and he loved my grandmother in the most wonderful way. They certainly had a beautiful marriage, even though my grandmother was the "head of the household," as she made most of the decisions and did all of the driving. They were so happy together and were a very good example of how two very different people can be so happy. He had a formidable family that included eight sisters. One died when she was young, but I knew all of the remaining seven sisters and they were all very likeable although they had very different personalities. It was like I had seven extra sets of grandparents, and I feel that this is where I developed my compassion and love and respect for older people that has been with me for my entire life. I learned to make them laugh and I listened to their stories of the past and really enjoyed getting to know them. So many times the retired and elderly are dismissed without any thought to their lives and the contributions they have made to their families and the wider world.

Can you imagine, my grandfather actually invited my great-grandmother to live with his family even though she was a mean-spirited woman who never missed an opportunity to vilify him! I witnessed this on many occasions. But the best example of this can be summed up in one memory I have as though it happened yesterday. I was about five or six and was staying with my grandparents while my brother and my parents were on a trip to Florida. I was playing happily and they both sat in the living room watching me. All of a sudden my grandfather brings out a nickel and says, "Why don't you go down to the corner store and buy yourself some candy." Well my great-grandmother then produced a dime and said, "You can't buy anything for that. Why don't you buy yourself an ice cream bar?" After that my grandfather said "Here is 30 cents; why don't you get yourself an ice cream and some candy." Where upon my great-grandmother pulled out 50 cents. At this point the yelling and competition between them was so bad I gave them their money back and told them I loved them both and did not want to be the object of their arguing. I was angry and I told them so. I also told them this was no way to behave in front of me. I know I was little but I felt that I had communicated to them what I felt they needed to hear. I don't believe that kind of incident occurred again. I believed they deserved to be embarrassed, especially my great-grandmother who started it. And I was proud that my usually docile grandfather had stayed in the fight.

My Aunt Alice was the one who introduced my mother and my father. My mother was teaching Sunday school with Aunt Alice, whose older brother, Herbert, had not had any serious relationships with women in his life. He was eight years older than my mother and was handsome and employed. He had a sense of humor (although rarely displayed to his children). I remember my mother had a beautiful garnet ring, her birthstone, and she told me that my father thought she would accept it as her engagement ring but she said no. So he did buy her a diamond engagement ring. My grandmother told me that her reaction to their engagement was profound, immediate, and angry. She said, "Please don't tell me that you are going to marry that small little man. You will never be happy."

My grandmother loathed my father from the beginning and felt that he was not worthy of my mother. She felt that he would never be able to provide for his family and had little potential to be a success at work or at home. But the wedding did take place on September 19, 1942. And this when our family began.

three

Our Family of Four

Our family started with the September 1942 marriage of our parents. After that, World War II began and Herbert enlisted in the Navy and was sent to the Pacific front. My father left with my mother pregnant with my brother who was born in August of 1944. My mother and brother lived with my grandparents until my father returned home. At that time my parents bought a typical Cape Cod style home like those that were being built all over in the suburbs after the G.I.'s came home. I was born in 1949. So here they were in suburbia with their two children, a boy and a girl, with life as a family ahead of them.

They joined a church and got involved in church activities and settled into the neighborhood where other young families had also moved. It was a typical 1950's setting where Mom stayed home with the children and Dad carpooled to work.

The house was a typical one from those days. It was a Cape Cod style with four rooms downstairs. They also finished the upstairs into three bedrooms, two of which were very small and had no closets or doors, just the old-fashioned, accordion-folding doors made out of vinyl. The two extra rooms downstairs were used as a dining room and the other as an office for my father. He wanted to become an insurance broker so he could ultimately quit his job at Prudential Insurance Company.

The property was great. It was a double lot so we had plenty of room to play. My father planted grapes along the back of the yard. We also had a large vegetable garden and a pear tree, a plum tree, and an apple tree. There were many bushes with beautiful flowers such as quince, honeysuckle, lilacs, and rose bushes of many types. We also had a flower garden filled with all kinds of wildflowers such as Queen Anne's lace, goldenrod, black eyed Susan's, and others.

Directly behind the house was a fenced-in area so we could be outside without supervision when we were younger. We even had an outdoor fountain that my father connected to the water faucet so we did not need to go into the house for a drink of water. In the middle of the play yard was a large maple tree that provided lots of shade.

If it sounds like our house setting was a peaceful and idyllic place to grow up, it was. There were lots of kids in the neighborhood and we all played together outside in the good weather. There was always someone to play with and something to do. In the winter we built igloos which were large enough to stand up in and were very warm. We could take off our coats and burrow out little shelves for candles so we could see. In the summer we ran through the sprinkler or went to the town lake to swim. I always felt safe and was very happy as was my brother. One of the boys in the neighborhood was my brother's best friend and is still his best friend today.

Doesn't it all sound so perfect?

The life that I have led and the peace that I have found in spite of everything and my desire to share with all of you reading this should stand as a single testament to the human spirit. I believe there is an unknowable number who, like me, have suffered and also gone on to live meaningful lives. It is now time for us to stand up and tell our stories so we can help future generations of children to avoid our struggles and to have people around us, especially our parents, to believe us and encourage children to tell their stories so that they can be safe while they are growing up.

four

The End of Our Family of Four

M y mother finally died at 95 on December 9, 2014. I guess we never know how we will feel at the death of a family member like my mother. Her death was actually like a weight being lifted off of me. I was 65 years old at the time. I don't remember anyone crying after she died. We just got through the funeral and the burial. She certainly was a difficult woman who was so self-centered. Prior to her death she had asked my brother and me if there was anything we wanted to know. We both said no. Then we told her we had been planning her service and she said she didn't want to know about it. She never said she loved us and we never said we loved her.

After her death our family spent weeks going through her place and ridding it of the many piles of things that had been just lying around. It was a painful and tedious process. When you go into someone's house to clean it out for sale and are responsible for all of someone else's possessions, it seems to be an insurmountable task. In this case every square inch of every area was covered. For example, she had an average-sized bedroom with a walk-in closet. In it were a single bed, a large dresser, two chests of drawers, a good-sized TV on top of a double-door cabinet, a living room chair with a side table, a telephone table, and a floor lamp. She also had something on top of and underneath everything in the room. Shoes were under each piece of furniture and clothes in boxes under the bed. This was just the bedroom. The walk-in closet in the room had three sides for hanging clothes and the floor and two shelves around the entire three sides of the closet. Every square inch was jammed with boxes, paper files, shoes in plastic boxes, and on and on. We threw out about 70 bags of junk and donated about 25 bags and boxes of assorted items. In addition we each took home at least 25 boxes. The boxes that we took home are filled with family photos and all sorts of items that could have some value. There was a great deal of jewelry and paperwork that could have historical value and letters that I wanted to read for this book. I was exhausted for so many reasons but especially from the realization that it was over for me. There would never be another chance for our entire family or for my mother, brother, and me to become a family. There would never be a chance for an apology or a hug or even an *I love you*. None of this happened and I can't remember if it ever had. An unfathomable and inestimable sadness came over me and made me cry and cry and cry. It just hurt me so much that I had missed out on my childhood, or rather, a normal childhood, and at the end I never even got a goodbye or an *I love you*. Or a hug. I cannot remember hugs in our family.

I remember clearly how I loved my children and there was never any doubt about that for them. As a family, we openly hugged and loved each other. It was obvious. There were many times when we told the children how much we loved them. My mother once asked me if I could tell her that I loved her and give her a hug. I don't think she ever truly showed that type of outward emotion to us. It was always difficult for me to comprehend her lack of emotion with her children because of the powerful emotions I felt for my children from the day they were born and they always knew that.

These deeply emotional feelings some time after her death kept reminding me of the day shortly before her death when I told my mother about the sexual abuse at the hand of my father, and she said,

"Oh, I didn't know anything about that." Then, after a few minutes of quiet, she looked at me in a strange and curious way and added, "You know, I never thought of your father as a particularly sexual person."

I answered that this was not about sex but about power. She never said another word, and after a several minutes of silence she just started another conversation like nothing had happened or was said. My brother was there with me when I brought up the subject of the abuse. As my brother sat there mute, I knew that my very last opportunity to bring some closure to this issue had failed, and I was once again shocked and devastated by the lack of compassion and honest discussion that existed in my family. My brother knew about the sexual abuse because I used to hide under his bed with my pillow some nights to stay out of my father's reach, but he had no comment or reaction. I don't believe we ever spoke directly about what had happened to me until I brought it up to him prior to my mother's death.

Some of you may have wondered about my brother and how what happened in our family affected him. I do know that the abuse I suffered had a profound effect on him. As I have said, my brother was a quiet, reserved child by nature. Outward signs of love from our parents probably would have been even more important for him but I do not know. I do know that the lack of open feelings for us hurt us both, even if in different ways. My brother is five years older than me. I love him with all of my heart. As a child he was always very quiet and calm and not a troublemaker. He was bright, an excellent student, and wonderful little boy. He was that perfect child that many of us wish for as parents and he was an absolutely wonderful brother to me. I was his crazy, wacky, exuberant little sister with the silly sense of humor and the curly red hair. He was a great brother, patient and kind to his whirlwind little sister. He couldn't have treated me any better and we were very close as children. We often played together and he brought me into his world with such things as showing me experiments with his chemistry set. We mixed the chemicals and used his Bunsen burner; our favorite concoction was rotten eggs. In the spring we would put gasoline in a metal bucket and went around our yard picking up caterpillars and plopping them in the bucket. We had a wonderful time watching them wriggle around and finally end up in a circle, dead. Then, we would set fire to the gasoline and watch them burn. We laughed together and had a very close relationship. When I was a little older he even let me play cards and games with his friends.

I remember one story during our childhood that is legendary. He was about fifteen years old and had been to a party at a friend's house. He was recounting the story of how his friend had been drinking shots at the party. I asked him (over and over) to show me what happened. We went to the liquor cabinet and used real liquor. Needless to say this prank did not end well and my brother got quite drunk. It was on a night when our mother was at a PTA meeting. I called my grandmother who lived two blocks from us at the time and she came right over. My mother was called at the school. By this time my brother was under the kitchen table and I was hiding in my bed.

As I said, my brother was very different from me. He was very intelligent but was always shy and quiet. He was very dependent on our parents and later on our mother. I know that he said that he never wanted to marry and have children. He felt that he was a slow worker and not proficient at his jobs and that he could not support a family. He held several jobs over the course of his life and was never truly happy at his work. He also talked about having many of the traits of my father. He reminded me that from 1964 after he graduated from college until my mother's death in 2014, he had spent every weekend with our parents unless he was travelling. His personality had changed dramatically from what it was like when we were children. He was still quiet and docile to the outside world. But, to his family, with whom he took out all of his frustrations regarding the wider world, he was very different.

While he was in college his insecurities and lack of self-confidence became more pronounced. The counselors there suggested that he should have counseling but, of course, my parents would never agree to that with what he knew about our childhood. During our normal conversations he would erupt into loud outbursts of anger. He would yell at all of us over the most insignificant things and later he would tell us that he couldn't help himself and we should just ignore these tantrums. He was very contrary and stubborn and opinionated. He criticized everything that everyone did in life and had all of the answers for how they could have done things better. But his own life was in many ways in tatters. He befriended people who had problems and helped them financially although he did not have the funds to spare. It was very heartbreaking for me to see him that way but, as hard as I tried, there was no way I could help him.

At this time after my mother's death I tried to be a mother to him and help him to "grow up" as if he was one of my children. This certainly wasn't my job. It is so difficult for me to think about how he lives his life now and how he has lived since he left his childhood home. I wanted to take on the task of mothering him as I truly wanted to help him to straighten out his house and to live what, by my standards, was a normal life but he had other ideas and did not want this help from me. This was hard on both of us but I finally realized that I had to let him be. I can't say that my brother or my brother's life was "normal" and I do know that he was deeply affected by the experiences of our childhood.

This conversation we had with our mother near her death haunted me for several days. I remember starting to feel like I wanted to commit suicide again. This was not the first time I had thought about suicide.

If this discussion seems out of order, it is, but I have something to say about suicide. I have a message for everyone who feels that suicide is an answer. I have felt suicidal on many, many occasions, too numerous to even estimate. By this I mean I having thoughts about relieving my feelings of hopelessness and despair at moments by ending my life. I don't mean actually planning this horrific act. But the first time I truly attempted suicide with a realistic plan was when I was twelve or thirteen, and we were at my aunt and uncle's home in New Hampshire and the four of us were sleeping together in the attic. I was totally creeped out because we were all sleeping in the same room. There were no walls to separate us and it was very uncomfortable to be sleeping in the same room with my father. I told my parents that I wanted to kill myself and they actually laughed at me. I told them that I was going to put a plastic bag over my head. They laughed even harder. They said something like, "Oh sure, like you could really do that." So, I put the plastic bag over my head and they never even came over to stop me. When I think about this incident I remember wishing at the time that I had the guts to do it. Boy that would have shown them. But they did not acknowledge my actions in any way except with their laughter. They never even came over to me to take possession of the plastic bag that I had over my head. I don't really remember what stopped me from doing it. By this time the sexual abuse had stopped. I guess in the end it was just my will to live that kept me alive and my love and trust in God, and my real hope that when I was able to chart my own life that I could find happiness and contentment. Yet, had I done it, this act would have shown the world a set of parents who were immersed in horrific grief over the death of their child from a senseless act, committed by an irrational child. The world would not have changed one iota by me doing this. But not doing it showed me something. It showed me that they did not care about me or what I did to myself. That I was on my own and that I could not count on them to care about me or to care for me. A very important lesson for me indeed. And one that I would NEVER forget. I believe this was the end of my hope that my parents would ever be there for me in my life.

As I said, I thought about killing myself many times and in many different ways. I certainly was in no way afraid of pain. My heart was so broken and my spirit was so desolate it really seemed like the only way out. Even when I had a husband who loved me and two wonderful little boys, I often felt that I wanted to die. You see, the will to live and the fight required not to commit suicide have nothing to do with the people around us and who love us. In my case it had to do with that terrible, awful thing that happened in the past. That thing from which there seemed to be no escape and the things that were said and done were so heinous that they could not be forgotten even after they were forgiven. There also seemed for a long time that there was no place to go to find help.

But then I think of the wonderful life I have had. During my childhood I was blessed with a grandmother who was my rock. She knew how to surround me with love, affection, security, and understanding. She was so strong, so funny and such an imp. She taught me how to survive hardship by her example. She was the one person who saved me throughout my childhood. Later in life I was blessed to have married a man who steadfastly loved me no matter what, two wonderful boys who grew up to be wonderful men with ethics and morals and integrity that are seldom seen anymore, my own business for 35 years, and all of the places I have travelled to and all of the wonderful people I have met and, of course, my beautiful (inside and out) daughters-in-law and the greatest gift of all, my two wonderful grandchildren.

Yes, I would have shown my parents had I done it but what I would have missed. At thirteen, I still had to be with them and essentially I belonged to them each and every day for about five more years, but then after that time I would be free of them. I could just ignore them as much as possible and do as I was told for the most part and I would be left alone.

At this time I also had my amazing grandmother so close by. I still think of her every day and have many things around the house that remind me of her. I also have her jewelry which I wear often and which always gives me strength. But the love, oh, the overwhelming love. It was love that was bottomless and enduring, even to this day, and of course it means so much to me, even after all of these years since she died. I still feel this love every day and draw on it for comfort, strength, and peace.

I am very much like her. She was always very strong and her example of how to live means so much to me. I have always felt that this saved me from even more horrors because I was strong like her.

By this time the abuse had stopped and I was at least free of that. I had learned to try to annoy my father as much as possible. That kept me sane. For example, at that time we had a parakeet. My father was

35

always well-dressed when he came home from work. He was very finicky and fastidious about his clothing, and, upon entering our home he would immediately go upstairs to change his clothes. My brother and I waited for him each day and immediately would let the bird out of his cage and the bird always made a beeline for my father's head. The bird loved rooting around in his hair. This upset my father but we did not care. And the treat was that many times Lucky would poop on his head or clothing. That was a special day for sure.

After working at my mother's house and on the estate paperwork for many days, I came home to my own messy house filled with at least 25 boxes and lots of dust. I had been so unhappy, so lonely and had neglected my own house. All of a sudden I was overwhelmed with an unbelievable grief over the death of my mother and our family. I was grieving so desperately that I could not get myself off the couch to make any progress, and I started to feel the old feelings of panic, inability to leave the house, loneliness, and most horrible, the depression and the insecurity.

Suicide was not the answer at this time. I had gotten to the point where I knew that. I want to share with you some of the reasons why suicide is never the answer. You have been brutally hurt by someone who took advantage of you as a helpless and frightened child. Your "inner child" is most likely calling the shots when you are hurt or depressed or bullied or mistreated in the present. Your "inner child" is the part of you who stopped growing emotionally at the age of the abuse. She endured the brutal childhood and feels there is no way to escape, even in the present. She is also the one who feels the powerful sting of the present and is not (or feels that she is not) powerful enough to go on. She cannot make the best decisions for the adult you. Her emotions are so real and so raw. This causes you to become that child again. And this child cannot make it without you the adult. She cannot stand up for herself. You are the one who will make this child whole again because in some ways you now have the perception and the process of an adult. In some ways…it takes a long time to get there.

Let's face it; you have been brutally hurt both physically and emotionally. But you need to know that you can make it. Suicide is not the answer. You deserve to have a life where you can thrive and know that you have value to you and to those around you. Your inner child has suffered enough. Help your inner child and try to help others who have had difficult times in their lives. I don't mean necessarily in a global way but even doing small things for people to help them means so much.

I try to remember how many times I wanted so badly to end my life. The last time I was very close to suicide was over 25 years ago. I was having a terrible time and was feeling so hurt by what had happened to me. The feelings had engulfed me in the moment because I was so tired from my work at the school and in the rest of my life. My son had been having a difficult time making friends and staying away from the boys who were not nice to him. After he got into high school he was in the band and then he tried out for the spring musical. He got the lead in the musical and this was wonderful. He was so pumped up about the performance and how he was accepted by his classmates as a "star." I felt he did not need me anymore and that my job as a mother was complete. My other son, while somewhat shy, was so together in most ways, and I felt that I could finally find the peace that had eluded me since I was eight years old. The boys were at a party with friends and family and I begged off because I was exhausted from the three-day production schedule. At that time I was very involved in the high school performing arts program as president of the Performing Arts Society. Our group decorated all of the venues such as the lobby and the cafeteria with items that reflected the plays or the musicals. I was also in charge of planning and decorating for a Friday night dinner in the cafeteria for family and friends of the performers plus an ice cream social for the Saturday matinee for area children and on Sunday a dinner for the senior citizens groups in our local towns, plus other activities in the lobby such as sales of refreshments during the intermissions. It was a huge responsibility and I loved it but it was very tiring. I was so proud of our son. He made many friends in the theater group and I felt that he was on his way to acceptance. I just wanted so badly to be at peace and to know that I would never have to suffer another panic attack or feel the misery of the memories that haunted me anymore. I also felt that my husband was such a wonderful father that the boys would be fine after they had recovered from the horrors of my death. I left the house in the car and headed to the beach and was planning to walk into the water and drown myself. Just like I had been in the water when I was three years old and my father saved me. I came home after several hours. The police were at the house when I got home. I had called my therapist who called back but I had already left the house. The therapist had told my husband to call the police and get them involved in finding me. My poor husband was a wreck and I promised him that I would not try it or consider it again. And I have stuck to that promise faithfully. And my sons, they needed me a great deal after that and I was always there for them. I was present in their lives and I could help them through the rough times and I was also present for the wonderful times. What we all would have missed if I had killed myself because of the horrors of my past!

Think about it; my will to live provided all of us with the lesson that life is so precious and priceless. And, to never ever forget that none of this was my fault or is your fault. Please remember that suicide will never let you reach the peace you so desperately need, want, and deserve. All it will do is end your life; that's it. It won't hurt anyone who did this to you. It won't "show them" what they did to you. It won't make them feel guilty for what they did to you. All it will do is to take away the life of another victim who can hopefully in the future fight for those poor children and others trapped in this life and bring them peace.

Take a moment to remember what you were like as an innocent eight-year-old child. You were most likely safe, loved, and protected by your family. Now try to put yourself in my place and imagine that you were me. Sexual abuse is a heinous crime and we need to stop it. And, remember this, when your child asks to speak to you, please give him or her your total attention. Telling you that this is happening to them is very difficult for a child. It takes an overwhelming level of trust between you and your child before he or she can directly tell you.

Also remember that when you become a parent, treat your children with love and respect no matter how they are behaving. Your main job as a parent is to bring your children up right so they can be productive members of society. No yelling, no hitting, no belittling them because they made a mistake. An example of this happened when my oldest son went to pre-school. When he came home I used to ask him what he did in school. I became very frustrated that he either couldn't remember or didn't want to take the time to tell me. One day I lost it and started screaming at him that we were paying for his school and he had to tell me. He looked at me like my head was spinning around and I realized what I had done. This was the same anger and hatred that I had seen from my father when he was abusing me. That was the last time that happened to me. From that point on I was able to be a parent and not a tyrant. After you have been abused, it is difficult to be a good parent but it is probably the most important thing you can do. It can and is a great way to turn around the cycle of abuse that is in your own family. Also remember that if you make a mistake in the way you have treated your child, you can and should sincerely apologize to them. This is another lesson that helps end the cycle of abuse. And it also teaches your children a very valuable lesson about openly apologizing when you are wrong.

I remember the time when my son was in the sixth grade and a male music teacher that he had met at a summer arts camp told me that my son was a talented musician and that he wanted to give him private lessons. I was thrilled about it but very wary. It took me a long time to make the decision. I asked many people who knew this music teacher and what did I find out? Many, many parents had asked him to teach their children but he only accepted the very best that he had personally selected. I felt very happy after I found that out from other parents. Our son learned a great deal from him BUT I never left my son alone with him and never strayed far from them while he was being taught in our home.

I read a staggering statistic recently that 40% of us have been abused in some way so this message is for every one of you. OPEN YOUR EYES! You are responsible for your child; and many times it is not the stranger with the dog, hiding in the bushes with candy, or luring your child into a car or into a public restroom. It is someone you know and has made himself or herself your friend whose personality belies his or her hidden sexual intentions. When our children were young we attended a well-established church in our town. The minister seemed like a very kind and good man and was also a good speaker who clearly conveyed God's message each Sunday from the pulpit. However, while Sunday school was in session before the church service (and when he was counseling youngsters in his office), he was in his church office sexually molesting young boys. He even kept a large cache of child pornography in his drop ceiling. One of the boys who was sent to the minister for counseling ran away from home, and the minister was able to tell the parents where he had gone because of his counseling sessions with the young man. Imagine how the parents must have felt when they found out about the sexual abuse that their son had endured at the hands of the minister, the same minister who conducted the funeral service for their son who had committed suicide.

To this day I have not been able to join a church and for many years I could barely enter a church due to the severe panic attacks that I endured after this came to light. This minister was in prison for a few years for these crimes, but no time is long enough as far as I am concerned when I think of the life these children lived after such horrors.

Our youngest son graduated from Pennsylvania State University. We absolutely loved the football program and for years wondered why Jerry Sandusky had left when he did. Of course we found out and what a tragedy that turned out to be. My thoughts are how many children could have been saved from him if only someone had cared enough to report this to the authorities so that these children could have received the help they needed and deserved.

There is also the boy who was molested by his Boy Scout leader. As a man he told me of his plight and that the leader was also his father's best friend. Think about it, all of these years the Boy Scout organization has refused to allow gay men to be leaders when this happened with a heterosexual family man who was a child molester.

It is always important to remember that children have no way to change their lives. You can and must be their protectors. Think about how, if something was happening to you as a child, you had no control over the situation. A child cannot move away from their family or change schools or move to a new house. The child's life is completely out of his or her hands. I am not saying this needs to change but it certainly needs to be taken into account. Never, ever let a child feel powerless! Never, ever let a child feel alone and without hope.

I also had an experience with our church minister when I was in the seventh grade. I told him about the terrible abuse by my father and he did nothing to help me. My father, after all, was one of the pillars of the church; and for this man of God, it was easier for him to look away from a youngster who was telling this "story" than to confront this pillar of his church. Just think of the repercussions this confrontation would have caused. Does this sound like something Jesus would have done? Of course not. Jesus gave his life for us in the most horrific way and this man of God could not even help a young lady who had been tortured by her own father.

I actually did forgive my parents and all through their lives I followed the fourth commandment, "Honor thy father and thy mother" even though it was so difficult. Remembering this reminds me of one time when my father was in the hospital. At the time I was in my late 30's. He had been sitting up in a chair and asked me to help him lie down. While helping him into bed he spread his legs and exposed himself to me. I must have had a horrified look on my face because he said to me, with a very large smirk on his face, "What's the matter? It's not like you haven't seen this before." He was probably 65 at the time. I was an adult with a family of my own, and yet, here I was a child again being abused by my own father after all of these years that had passed. This is the power of the abuse that normal people rightly have an extremely difficult time understanding.

Believe in yourself and know that you are valuable regardless of what you have suffered. Know what your "pressure points" are so you can control them or at least understand them. For example, when I was in a room and I smelled a pipe burning or heard a single violinist playing, I completely freaked out and immediately had a panic attack because my father was a pipe smoker and played the violin. However, after I realized this, I was able to get over this freaky response to these two triggers.

Never forget that your will to live is not a cruel punishment but a priceless gift, and you deserve to live and thrive. You matter and you are an important member of society and you have a message for the public at large and for individuals with whom you have a relationship. You can do so much to help others. Learn to get through the hard times so you can feel the joy of life.

And, if you are the person who is honored to be there for your wounded inner child, always know that you are a treasure and your difficult task is worth the hard work you endure. For you will also have the privilege to share in the wonderful times as you, your partner, and or your friends are able to work toward having your inner child grow up and recover and survive.

five

The First Time

One night when I was eight years old and in a deep sleep I sensed someone in my bedroom. My father had come in very quietly. He seemed calm to me. I stirred awake as he stood before me with his pajama bottoms removed. As I awoke further I was shocked and very frightened by what I saw. He smiled at me with an evil smirk and pulled up my nightgown. In order to secure his way into me, he climbed up on my bed and put his right leg on my left leg with my knee bent and my hip turned for his easier entry. His left hand held both of my arms back and over my head and his right hand was placed over my mouth. I did not struggle because it was my father and I was half asleep and did not know what was happening. Remember I was eight years old at the time. He forced himself into my body and raped me. When it was over he left saying nothing and went back to his bedroom where my mom was no doubt peacefully sleeping through the rape of her eight-year-old daughter.

The next morning when I awoke what happened a few hours before almost seemed like a dream or, better said, a nightmare.

In those days we only had one bathroom in our home. My father was shaving when I went downstairs to use the toilet. As I sat on the toilet I looked up at my father and stared at him and he said to me testily "What are you looking at?"

It was beginning to sink in on some level what had happened to me. The bond of trust between us was broken. I began to feel that he was the devil, an evil being, with as much understanding as an eight-year-old child could have. His manner was demonic; he stared at me through eyes that had a look of power and an understanding that he could use that power. He had finally freed himself from his prison and found his release.

The rest of the morning at home was ludicrously normal. We all got dressed and ready for the day. Dad went to work and we got ready for school. I expected someone to say something after Dad left. No one said anything. It was so unreal. I don't know how to explain it except that I thought someone would help me, tell me what to do, I don't know what. But, no, just a regular day. A regular day—just take a moment to wrap your mind around that.

In those few minutes of his powerful abuse I had changed forever. FOREVER. No matter what I did for myself to feel better, to get over what had happened I would rocket back to that terrible place again and again. I could never forget those terrible minutes and I never found peace. It was never to be the case. The most disturbing part of my life would re-occur over and over whenever something happened that reminded me of his demeanor, his power, his arrogance, his complete domination of me, the way he made me feel useless and unloved, like something not worthy to spit on or to use to line the garbage can. I was a person for his pleasure. I felt useless and thrown aside with no pride or self-worth. Like I was being thrown in a mud puddle or in a lake or off of a boat or over a cliff or under a train or out of a plane or into a den of hungry lions.

I ask you now to remember I was eight years old. An innocent eight-year-old girl who would never be normal ever again. Who would never act the same, feel the same, or be like any other eight-year-old. My life was ruined by the sins of commission by my father and the sins of omission by my mother. All of the "normal" days that followed were never normal to me again. Never, not ever, not for one day. I had changed forever and was hurt, violated, and incapable of ever being like others who were my age and had not suffered as I had.

From then on nothing I did, for many years, felt worthy. I was a piece of garbage. I was changed at eight years old in major ways. From that point on I had no feelings of self-worth. This made it very difficult to make friends because I tried too hard never feeling worthy of friendship. I also never felt that I could trust anyone. When you are a child and you can't trust your parents, who can you trust? The only people that I felt a kinship with were those who also were struggling in their lives for various reasons. Years ago we used the expression "friend of the friendless" and that was me. Even as a young child I suffered from suicidal ideation and thought not about actually killing myself but how wonderful it would be to be dead. And maybe the saddest part of my young life was that I never found anyone who could or would hear me.

I also became a real overachiever in school and elsewhere in my life because I needed to be the best. The best of the best to make up for how I knew I was really nothing. In addition, studying and reading would keep me buried in information and away from my thoughts.

This was the pattern for my life. In my early years I always had straight A's on my report cards. In fifth grade I won the reading contest for reading the most books in my class. I still have the little fawn pins that the teacher awarded to me. Even today when I look at them I can remember how proud I felt of that achievement. But I was so troubled in school and even looked for a teacher who I could tell; I never did find that person. So I decided to act out to get attention. But even that did not work.

In fourth grade I tried to get attention by stealing my friend's wallet. She was very upset and the teacher asked us to please look around and ask around to see if we could find it. I couldn't take it and I put it back in her desk when no one was looking. I just couldn't be the bad guy and hurt anyone, even if it ruined my chance to be reprimanded and be alone with an adult I could tell what was happening to me.

In the third grade I had a wonderful teacher whom I loved and I thought I had finally found someone whom I could tell. Unfortunately she was out for a few months because she needed surgery. So our class had a substitute. I still wanted someone to notice me so I decided I would write with my left hand. My writing was atrocious but I was never pulled out of class so I could tell my story. When my permanent teacher came back to school one day I pretended I was sick to my stomach and threw down a fake plastic puke on the floor. The teacher called for the custodian to clean it up. But even my charade was not enough to get me in trouble and in a conference with someone who might listen to me. I did not know how to be a discipline problem. All of my attempts to be bad were in vain. I also dreamt often that I could fly. I wouldn't go to far off beautiful lands but just to the telephone pole next to our property just so I was out of my father's reach. For the little me it was a piece of heaven to be safe and away from his grasp and the horror of my childhood.

My grandmother and great-grandmother moved to our town and lived only two blocks away from us. When I attended middle school, their house was on my way home so I stopped at their house almost every day after school and many evenings I had dinner there. Being with my grandmother was always good for me and I loved her cooking and also watching her cook. And her warmth…she always hugged me and told me that she loved me! My mother and father never commented on why I wanted to spend so much of my time there. As a mother I certainly would have wanted to know why my child did not want to be with me.

As I mentioned earlier our family were Christians. I even have my Sunday school pin to show that I had eight years of perfect attendance. My father was very involved in the church. Many years later I was speaking to the minister who married my husband and me and was a friend of our family. His family attended our church before he went to the seminary to become a minister. He laughed about my father and how he always had way-out ideas and was not respected by anyone. He even told me that the rest of the people my father worked with at the church also laughed at him and ridiculed him behind his back. This was a man whom I had known since before the abuse began and I never told him what had happened to me.

I loved my church youth leaders and accepted Jesus Christ as my savior when I was in the seventh grade. The minister in those days was much younger than when we first attended church there. As I said earlier, I took a chance telling him but to no avail. He looked at me and seemed incredulous and chose to tell me that I must be wrong. The amazing part of this is that I was able to follow the Ten Commandants with no compunction and, for the most part, treated my parents with respect and helped them both as they aged. In fact my father had Parkinson's disease and wanted to participate in a drug trial project that was one hour from our home and I drove my parents there and back every week. I also had to bring my very young children with us. It was rather grueling, but he wanted to go and I saw that he got there for many weeks before he became too ill to continue.

Like so many of us, I had very different political and social interests from my parents. However, I always felt that they were fair because they were religious. I never expected them to act inappropriately with regard to social issues. A perfect example of this would be when I chose a black roommate my sophomore year in college. They were horrified. Here I went to church all these years and was taught how to treat people and they were shocked and dismayed by my choice. After high school I never listened to them or sought their opinion.

I participated in many of the normal high school activities. Remember I did not want to be at home. I joined the debate team and the forensic society and loved it. I think what helped me the most was having to argue on both sides of the issues. That was truly a learning experience and shaped my ability as an adult to talk to and with people; no matter what their circumstances or ideas I could understand and show respect for their side of an argument.

Learning to show respect for someone who holds a different point of view in life is very important. We need to understand where others are coming from and what life experiences they have had that have molded their reactions and feelings about certain issues in life. This will help us all to be better people. It will also help us to stand up to people who have different ideas and values because we understand their thoughts on these volatile subjects. We can also learn the triggers that upset others and avoid these triggers in order to keep the peace. With practice (as in don't give up) we can be in a good place ourselves and help others to be there at the same time. These coping skills are especially important to understand and practice with people such as family members that we cannot escape.

I was also the student director of our school drama production. By some awful co-incidence the teacher who was the director was fired years later for molesting young boys. In addition I was also a member of the school honor society and the yearbook staff.

I loved all of my subjects in school…English, history, Spanish, Latin and economics. But not math. I remember having no problems with algebra but then there was the year I took geometry. For one test, the teacher, who knew how hard I worked, asked the class how long each of them had studied for the test. Would you believe that I studied more than all of the other kids added together and still got the lowest grade! Fortunately for me the teacher took pity on me and I passed with a C for effort. I'm pretty sure that was the only C I got in school.

And so I managed to graduate from high school in reasonable condition except for the ulcer that I had in my senior year. One day Ken's buddies were driving from the University of Maryland to New York City and they agreed to drop him off at our home for a visit. I was so happy to see him but I was really miserable at the time. His visit was such a blessing. He always had a way to make me feel lighter. I don't know that I recovered any sooner but at least it was a respite that kept me from spiraling even further into the abyss. I continued to do what the doctor had recommended and fortunately the ulcer was soon in my past. I now understand that the ulcer was a direct result of the sexual abuse just showing up in my body in a different way.

six

My Inner Child

In those first few minutes of the initial sexual abuse at the hands of my father I had changed forever. No matter what I did for myself to feel better, to get over what had happened, it was never to be. The most disturbing part of my life would be the involuntary reflex that rocketed me back to that terrible time and place whenever something happened that reminded me of his demeanor, his power, and his abuse. This is something that those of you who have never felt the horror of sexual abuse need to understand.

For victims of sexual abuse, this is where your inner child takes hold of your life. As I grew older there was a part of me that never did grow up. Try to understand what happened to me. There is so much shame for survivors of sexual abuse and it is debilitating for those of us who feel it. In one brief moment in time your feet are kicked out from under you. And no one comes to help you. People just stand around and look at you like you are a piece of garbage. My heart was broken and my spirit was destitute. I wish I could put this pain into words so that you could understand this pain that lasts a lifetime.

In addition to how terrible the sexual abuse was to endure from my father at age eight years old, remember that my mother was incapable of helping me with any emotional issues in my childhood. Her inability to help me and my brother as well only exacerbated my lack of feelings of self-worth and my struggles to grow into a complete person in adulthood. The moment I felt that something bad happened to me it was like being violated again by my father. These feelings came to me again and again. I was unable to stand up for myself with anyone. I tried so hard to find some way to understand life in general, and my life in particular, but it was impossible under the circumstances.

For example, when I was younger I used to sit in my parents' dark closet with the door closed and hold my father's soft and warm bathrobe close to my face in an effort to negate what my father had done. As I got older I tried to find other ways to cope with my insecurities but it was so difficult. Actually, until I had therapy it was all but impossible.

As the years of your life pass you grow from an infant to a toddler to a kindergartner, to an elementary school and middle-school student, and finally you graduate from high school. For the child who has not been abused you are able to develop a sense of self, you begin to find out who you are and to grow up hopefully as a whole and intact adult. You learn how to deal with situations like having a friend move away or having a close relative die. You also experience disappointments, such as not getting on the team or not getting the part in the play. Children who are fortunate to have loving and responsible parental relationships are taught how to get through these sad, tragic or disappointing events. Sometimes a child has someone else in his life who is there to help.

But, as victims of childhood sexual abuse, our inner child never grows up and never learns about feelings and emotions and how to handle them on an adult level. We only function on the level of the age and maturity of our inner child at the time we were a victim. There is no emotional growth past that point. Imagine never going through these stages of life and growth. All of these stages are different and different skills will be mastered as we grow along the way. For example, we mature; we learn how to deal with our peers, our siblings, our parents, our grandparents, our teachers and others while we are growing up. Some of our experiences are good and some are not so good. We can be exhilarated by some and discouraged by others. But all of our experiences add up to the adults we become.

People who experience trauma and abuse at a young age are almost stopped at that age (in my case eight years old) from learning how to cope with life. We remain at the emotional maturity of a child. We do not develop life skills as others do which is why, for example, I developed severe panic attacks as I did not have the capacity and understanding needed to cope with these normal situations of adulthood. The fact that we cannot grow and prosper is because the child within us never grew up and is still a child with childlike reactions to our surroundings. We are small, young children who have to deal with older children, teenagers, and adults but we are incapable of doing so because of our stunted emotional growth.

I believe this lack of ability to understand life on an adult level at times has been the most difficult part of my life and the most difficult part or the strangest part for adult friends and relatives to understand. One moment I would be an adult talking to someone, but if something was said or something happened that brought me back to the past I changed, my entire demeanor changed, and no one could understand what had happened to me. All of a sudden I was that child again experiencing these terrifying feelings of being abused.

So, after that first time I experienced the abuse, I still believed in myself and thought and thought about ways to make it stop. I decided that if I talked to my father rationally, I could make him understand that I wanted him to stop. Think about what I am saying here. As an eight-year-old I confronted my father! One day we were alone in the house and I hatched a plan. I would talk to him quietly and rationally and explain how much it was hurting me and ask him to stop. After all, he was my father and he loved me, right? Wasn't that the way it worked? I was a voracious reader, even at this young age, and all of the books I read started with a situation or a problem and the people in the story worked to correct whatever was wrong and everyone was smiling at the end. It seemed reasonable to me that I could use tactics such as these to have a discussion with my father and this would be the way to proceed. I have come to realize how mature I was at only eight years old in order to be able to reason like this.

My father, who always hated his job at the Prudential Insurance Company, had recently gotten an insurance license and was trying to sell property and casualty insurance on the side as a way to be able to leave his job at the Pru. To this end, we had converted one of the rooms in our home to his office. One day when the two of us were home alone I found him there sitting at his desk when I asked to speak to him.

I asked him to stop hurting me.

As he stood up and with all of the quiet anger he could muster, he told me in no uncertain words that I was a nobody and that nobody cared about me. After he stood up, he leaned towards me, slapped his desk with real fury and said, "I don't love you, nobody loves you, and nobody will ever love you. And I will do whatever I want to you."

And so the abuse continued from there for several more years. And the trauma would continue forever.

But my story will show how I used this experience to mold my personality to help many others, including my children, to have power in their lives.

seven

My Early Romance and the Trip to Guatemala

We moved from Pequannock, New Jersey, to Fair Haven, New Jersey, in the fall of 1964 when I was 15 years old and a sophomore in high school. My uncle Bill, who also worked at the Prudential Insurance Company as a mortgage loan appraiser, was working in the Fair Haven area and told my parents about how beautiful the area was. They travelled to Fair Haven to see the area and found a lot and house plans for a home that could be built to their liking. Since my great-grandmother had died and my grandmother was ill, she was moving to Fair Haven as well and would be living with us.

The contractor began to build the house in the summer and it was finished in October of 1964. I had never moved before and, with my background, I could have been very upset about moving. It would mean starting an entire new life and trying to make friends. But the funniest thing happened. I had been registered for the high school as of the first day of the school year as a sophomore but, as I said, the house was not finished until October. Since the beginning of the school year everyone had been waiting for me. It had become the mystery of the school year in my classes…where is this new student and when will she get here. The students were all excited when I finally arrived on the scene. In some of the classes I was surrounded by smiling students, some classes cheered when I arrived, and some of them clapped. It was probably one of the nicest arrivals for a new student!

Things continued to go well for me. I did make some friends which was great. I liked it there and was happy with the move and living with my grandmother whose bedroom was right across the hall from mine.

One day when I was fifteen, one of my new friends said she knew a nice guy and she would like to introduce him to me and perhaps we could go on a double date. His name was Ken. We went out on a Saturday night shortly after that. Ken drove the car which I later found out belonged to the other young man's brother! I guess he was trying to impress me. We went to see the movie *Mary Poppins* at the Paramount Theatre in Asbury Park, NJ. When I got home my mother asked me how the date was and I answered with a smile, "It was all right." Not a very impressive reaction to say the least. Then I got to know Ken. He was just an all-around nice guy. He was fun and lighthearted and he brought joy into my life with his beautiful smile and his great sense of humor. And not just joy but a true feeling that he was someone who had nothing to be unhappy or restless or uneasy about. He just seemed weightless. He was intelligent and grounded. I never met anyone like him in my life. It was as though he didn't have anything heavy on his heart. He didn't complain about things in life and he just was always content. My immediate family was filled with moaners, complainers, and my parents were never satisfied with anything—I mean anything.

Whatever they bought, whether big or small, work done on the house, anything and everything, it was not good enough. To illustrate this I used to tell my friends that when my parents bought a new car, they found six things wrong with it by the time they got home. One of my friends once retorted I should be happy we didn't live farther from the car dealership.

The life I lived and my heavy heart were so different. Ken was a jewel. Did I love him? That took a very long time as I had already decided that I never wanted to marry. Never once did he pressure me or ask me for more than I could give. I don't remember when I first told him I loved him and he never asked me or pressured me about it.

When I met him he was a senior in high school and I was a sophomore. I remember that my locker was at one end of the school near my math class. I didn't know it at the time but he used to run down there after his class on the second floor of the old building so he could be casually waiting for me after class looking cool and relaxed when I emerged from my class. He always greeted me with a great big smile.

When we remember those days so long ago, several funny stories come back to us. Once when we were on the beach and laughing together I got up to run away. He ran after me and reached out and grabbed my foot. I went down hard, face first in the sand. When I got up he was worried I would be angry but I just laughed and laughed. He lightened my spirit every time I was with him. It was heavenly! Another time we were in the car at the local ice cream hangout. We were enjoying our ice cream when I noticed he was looking at the girl in the car next to ours. I put my ice cream cone next to his face and called his name. His head swung around and his cheek smacked into the ice cream. And we laughed and laughed. I was having fun for the first time in my life. I am a very competitive person. We used to play cards at the beach and I could never figure out how he could beat me with every hand until he confessed that he was reading my cards from the reflection off of my sunglasses. But even when he "got me" it was with a huge grin on his face. What a bright, shining light.

He soon became a fixture in our house. I remember that I told him he could get his own drinks from the refrigerator. My grandmother, who was a pip said, in a stage whisper, "Why is that boy going into our refrigerator?" One of the neighbors called him a mustard plaster. He would say, "Is that mustard plaster at your house again?"

Over the years he met my entire family including eight aunts and uncles and my eleven cousins. Everyone liked him. He was like a big teddy bear, ready to hug the world and full of smiles and good thoughts.

Just knowing him changed me so much. I never knew that people like him existed in the world. He was open and happy and fun. One thing he wasn't was pushy. He never tried to coerce me to do anything I wasn't interested in doing. Nor did he partake in activities I didn't approve of such as drugs or excessive alcohol. We did smoke, however. We enjoyed going to our high school teen canteen on Friday nights during the school year. There were movies, basketball, dancing, ping pong, and probably a few other activities we have forgotten. Many of the students took advantage of the teen canteen and it was always well attended. We had our first kiss at Teen Canteen during a movie. It was interrupted by one of our teachers, Mr. Bain, our geometry teacher. It's another memory we love! In those days we didn't have money to go out so this was a good alternative. We also went to house parties. Generally these were when parents were not around, but we never stayed for the late-night shenanigans such as people going upstairs and stealing things, putting cigarettes out on hardwood floors, someone dancing, or crashing into and knocking over a china cabinet that held treasures from European travels.

We went to the beach or the movies most of the time or we spent time at my house. Of course he loved my grandmother. I don't really remember any conversations between Ken and my father and/or my mother. Yes, they exchanged pleasantries but that was all. They really weren't interested in knowing anything about him. All was well; there didn't seem to be any problems that they needed to be concerned about so they were satisfied.

My grandmother was different. She and I talked about him and our relationship all of the time. She asked about him, about his family, where he would go to college and on and on. My grandmother was also very fun loving and would tease me at every opportunity. One day she asked me what we did when we were out in the car Ken drove, which was a small Renault. "So, what do you do when you go out with him in his car?" I finally said with exasperation the car was so small it was impossible to do anything in it. "Oh," she said, not missing a beat, "I thought you got out and rolled in the grass." That was my granny!

In the spring of my sophomore year, my aunt and uncle asked my parents and me if I would like to be an exchange student in Guatemala. There was nothing more that I wanted to do than leave my life with my parents and be able to visit a foreign land on my own. This was one of the most important times in my life and absolutely changed my life forever. I could not wait to leave and to be away on my own!

My cousin Judy had been an exchange student in Guatemala, and the family she stayed with had a daughter my age. The Guatemalan family wanted me to travel there to live with them for several months, and then their daughter would come stay with us in the United States. I was absolutely thrilled! I would be leaving my family and travelling all the way to Guatemala by myself. These would also be my first airplane flights. I flew out of JFK airport to New Orleans and on to Guatemala City, the capital of Guatemala. You should have seen the outfit I wore. It was a bright yellow dress and heels with a wacky yellow high hat with white gloves and a pocketbook. Travelling was very different in those days. On the plane to Guatemala I met an American businessman who listened to my story. He was very helpful and looked at the photos of the Gularte family. I had told him that I had never met the family. When we arrived he stayed with me until he saw that I had safely met the family. I've never forgotten that kindness. Then he just quietly slipped away. I turned to thank him but he was gone.

My sweet Ken did not object to me leaving in any way. Actually, he told me after the fact I didn't ask or share this opportunity with him. I just said, "Oh, I am going to Guatemala and will be leaving in early July and returning in mid-October." By this time in our short relationship he already realized that I was independent and would do as I pleased. I never asked him if he minded me leaving him. That would have never occurred to me. And if I lost him because of the separation, that would have been his decision! I would have never given up this opportunity for him. I wanted to take advantage of this opportunity to travel to Guatemala to live in another culture and absorb more knowledge about the world and how different other cultures were.

Even though I was only sixteen I was already open to new and daring experiences in my life. I can't say that I missed my parents at all. Would Ken still be my boyfriend when I returned home? Only time would tell and I would never have given up this amazing adventure even if it meant losing him. For Ken, it was probably his first experience with my independence and how I would not change the course of my life or give up opportunities for him. I have always been grateful that he has accepted me just the way I am and he loved my independent spirit.

Guatemala… an absolutely magical experience. I just loved it there. Their house was lovely and comfortable but certainly not luxurious by today's standards. It had a combination living room/dining room, several bedrooms, and a kitchen, along with quarters for the maid. It was surrounded by a stucco fence and I don't remember much of a yard. Mr. Gularte was a Guatemalan senator and Mrs. Gularte was a stay-at-home Mom. Marlene, their daughter, who was my age, had three older sisters, Aura Marina, Myrna, and Mireya. None of them lived in the house and they were all married. She also had a younger brother Abel, who was not a natural child of the Gulartes. He was about twelve. At the time I arrived Marlene was at the Worldwide Girl Scout Jamboree in Idaho and would be returning in two weeks. I was lonely without her but I survived just fine.

Mr. Gularte felt it was his duty to help me learn to speak Spanish. I had only had two years of Spanish in high school and it was not really conversational Spanish. I had a long way to go. But I learned something else about myself and that was that I had a very easy time picking up the Spanish language along with the accent. I remember most of all sitting at the dinner table with Mr. Gularte pointing to everything on the table and asking me to repeat it. As time went on he expanded his task to include household items and then social words so I could master the gist of the language. I picked it up very quickly and was really fluent in about two months. Not every word in the language but certainly enough for social situations.

In reading my Guatemalan diary I found all of the characteristics that had been part of my life since the childhood abuse. My interactions with others were all over the place. I had a problem in the beginning of the trip because Marlene was away for two weeks. The Gulartes kept me very busy with social engagements with their children and friends. Most of the time I had something to do but it was still difficult for me to have so much free time. I also spent much time agonizing over the length of time it took to receive a letter…eight days. I was constantly angry and then forgiving about how long it took for Ken's letters to arrive.

After Marlene came home we attended school, and it was a first for me to wear a uniform. I did not find the school to be anywhere equal to ours in the United States, but they did attend more years of college, which I'm sure made quite a difference in their education. I couldn't say the students at Maria Auxiliadora were intellectuals like Marlene and me, but they were absolutely lovely young women and very kind and good to me. I did attend many parties when I was there and the young people knew how to have a good time. The parties were really dances and I mention in my diary dancing from 7 p.m. until 11 p.m. without a break. I do remember one party where one of the young men told me the food I was eating was dog meat. It never fazed me but Mr. Gularte had a talk with him!

In addition we did a great deal of travelling. Guatemala is a breathtaking country filled with ancient history, beautiful natural settings, and interesting people and crafts. I still have many of the things I brought back with me around my home. We visited Antigua, Guatemala, the old capital that was destroyed by an earthquake in 1773 and that was built and settled by the Spaniards. It was never rebuilt because it stood for the old Guatemala which people wanted to forget. The city of Chichicastenango has a beautiful marketplace filled with many crafts and an ancient Catholic Church at which the Indians have melded their pagan rituals with Catholicism. We visited

Lake Atitlan with its volcano at the edge of the lake. At the right time of day you can see the reflection of the entire volcano in the lake. Lake Amatitlán is also a beautiful Guatemalan lake. We took a school trip to Quetzaltenango leaving at 3 a.m. and returning at 11p .m. What a long day! It is a beautiful typical Guatemalan city with the old and new mixed together and of course the beautiful scenery. The Gulartes also took me to Tapachula, Mexico to swim in the Pacific Ocean and to experience a black sand beach. I was amazed by the height of the palm trees. And we travelled to San Salvador, El Salvador.

But one of my favorite days from a humanistic perspective was when I went on a bus with Chila, the family maid, to her village, Chimaltenango. It was about 35 miles from Guatemala City via a heart-stopping winding road filled with many pot holes. When we arrived at the village of Chimaltenango, it was quite an experience. The villagers had never seen someone with red hair. At the time my hair was quite long. They flocked around me and in a very courteous way smiled at me and motioned to me to ask if it would be okay to touch it. It was fun and everyone was smiling. Then Chila took me to see her home. It was a one-room home with sparse furnishings and a dirt floor. The dirt was very packed down so it almost looked like a manufactured floor. I will cherish that outing always because, for a young American, it was eye-opening to see life lived in that old-world way. They did not have many worldly possessions but they were happy. It was an unbelievable and valuable experience for a young lady from America.

One of the other interesting adventures that I was able to have was to go to a real rock-em/sock-em wrestling match between Huracan (Hurricane) Ramirez and Frank Carnicero (Butcher). I loved those crazy experiences as much as the cultural ones. I was accompanied by Moises, who was a friend of the Gularte family so they knew I would be safe. I also went to a Congressional gala where I was introduced to El Presidente de Guatemala. That was quite special also. And I had the opportunity through the government contacts to meet two American military couples that had just arrived to begin serving their time stationed in Guatemala. Talk about two ends of the spectrum.

My letters home (which my mother kept) were so interesting to read, but all of these years later most interesting to me is how I felt there. I was very happy with the family and Marlene and my social life, but I did have many times where I felt uncomfortable, not wanted, and that I did not fit in. My interactions with people did not change and, as usual, I muddled through being on my way to adulthood but I still felt serious insecurities. I do know that I was immensely happy to be away from home.

In retrospect it was a fabulous time. I know this is where my love of travel started, which has certainly been a gift to me and Ken and our children. I arrived home in mid-October and got right back to my studies. It was strange because I really had trouble speaking English at first. Marlene arrived before Christmas, and I feel that she enjoyed herself in this country as well. We took her to see places in the US such as the Empire State Building, the Statue of Liberty, and the sights in Philadelphia and other places. She liked Ken immensely and was thrilled when he invited her to Christmas shop for me. Together they picked out a lovely double pearl ring that is safely tucked away in my jewelry box. We also both remember the first time she was introduced to ice. We were heading out to the parking lot and saw the moisture on the ground. We told her to be careful of the ice, but the next thing we knew she was on the ground. It was such a shock to her and thankfully she was fine. We got along very well at our house. She attended school with me and seemed to be contented with the arrangements and travel plans while she was with us. Of course there was a bond between us that was very strong. And we kept in touch with each other, but less and less as our educational goals and family goals continued to increase as we got older.

Unfortunately this is not the end of the story. A few years after Marlene went back home and completed her studies, she was married and had two children. Her husband was an attorney who was very involved in Guatemala helping the Indian people who had been held down for so long and were not able to progress. At that time there were many guerrilla forces who did not want the Indians to flourish and prosper. Marlene's husband, Roberto, was captured and killed by the guerilla forces. His body was never discovered or returned to the family. Marlene was pregnant with their third child when she was taken by the guerilla forces. Her body was finally found after a long search by her siblings. She was found in a warehouse filled with dead bodies. There were hundreds of bodies there, but her sister Mireya kept searching through the stench and the heat until she found Marlene with her face smashed in and the baby cut out of her body. Mireya was able to identify her by her jewelry.

So ends the beauty and peace of my first pilgrimage away from home.

eight

The College Years

After Marlene left my life returned to that of a normal high-school student. With one big exception...I developed an ulcer which was certainly a portent of the life of more problems that were closing in around me. There was always that nagging belief I had that something was inherently wrong with me. It crept up on me slowly and insidiously, but my courage and my fortitude never failed, although at times they did waiver. I knew there were serious issues in my life but had no skills to deal with them, so I learned to cope as best I could and to survive until I could extract myself from the toxic relationships that I had with my parents.

In school I was involved in the Forensic Society (public speaking, dramatic presentations, and debate) for the remainder of my high-school years and continued to enter many competitions, and, I remember that I was quite a good public speaker by the time I graduated. Public speaking is a wonderful thing to become familiar with since so many people are very frightened of it. I also was involved with the yearbook. In our senior year we decided to have quotes under each senior picture and I worked diligently on that project. Mine was, "Speech is the twin of my vision; it is unequal to measure itself," which was chosen for me by another senior. This quote comes from Walt Whitman's *Leaves of Grass* "Song of Myself" from section 25. In addition I was a member of the National Honor Society. Of course then came the difficult decision as to where to go to college. I was accepted to two schools and had made my decision, but I kept thinking about a private women's college in Chambersburg, Pennsylvania, that my guidance counselor had spoken about at great length. It was Wilson College which soon became the second love of my life.

Things were so different in those days. I never saw the school until I arrived on campus there. But I loved the beautiful campus on sight as soon as I arrived. I also loved my room and my roommate, and we became very dear friends over time. I remember our first encounter, standing in line to get my dorm and room assignment and realizing that the person standing in line next to me was going to be my roommate! I smiled at her and she looked back at me as though trying to size me up in that brief moment in time. I had a scholarship for one-third of the cost from the college, a New Jersey state scholarship for one-third of the cost (for two years), some help from my parents and the rest of the expense was via loans to be paid back by me. I remember at the time of acceptance my mother telling me that my father made $6000 per year and the cost of the school was half of his annual salary. I was grateful in my own way for their help to attend school there and remember the great relief that flooded over me when my mother told me that I could go to Wilson.

I loved it there with all of my heart, and I will never forget breakfast on the morning I left for school. I ate with my parents who were both taking me to Chambersburg and I said to them, "Just think, this is the last time that I will sit at this table and think of this as my house. I am starting my own life now." It was a life-changing time for me and all for the better. Or so I thought. It is never good to know what is coming in life. The future for me would be filled with many horrific times. But not at the time I was beginning my college journey. I enjoyed every day there to the fullest and dealt with the bad things that came along when they arrived at my doorstep.

I loved college. I loved my room. I loved the girls. I loved my classes. I loved my roommate. I loved the view from my window on the ground floor looking out onto the grass and the woods. I loved the campus. I loved the politics. I loved walking downtown. It was a very small college with about 1,250 women students. Aside from my studies I became involved with the college radio station as a deejay and eventually became the station manager. I just enjoyed it so much. I have gone back to Wilson College for my 25th, 40th and 45th reunions and had a great time. One thing that was brought up at our reunions was how so many of us grew up in Republican homes but changed our politics while we were there, becoming Democrats. That describes what happened to me. This was significant because it describes the changing social and political times of the late 1960's.

In the first two years I took all of the required courses including basic math. I especially mention this course because the professor started our first class by telling us he was not happy he had to teach a basic math course to non-math majors. I believe the term he used was unequipped young ladies. I mention this because my main career was totally math-based as I was a financial and income tax professional. Of course this career used "basic math" and did not include calculus or other advanced mathematical studies. I never felt sorry for this obviously annoyed professor.

Late in my sophomore year I decided to select two majors, economics and sociology, with a minor in education. One thing that was so great about Wilson was the classes that we had with our professors once we had selected our major. The group of economics majors in my class numbered six, and we had two economics professors who were wonderful and very helpful during our studies. We met with them often and I'll never forget what one professor said to me, "You know, Shirley, I have heard you talk about everyone in your family except your father." Later in life this remark came back to me more than once. This professor and I were close and he was always caring and helpful as was my other economics professor. I really enjoyed our relationships. It was indeed unusual for a woman to major in economics in those days, but I truly loved it and was extremely content with my choice, which definitely served me well.

With two majors and a minor that meant that I really had no elective courses except for those in my majors and minor. These courses were based highly on reading and writing, and my economics major included a comprehensive exam before I could pass my major course of study. But I loved the work and thrived in the environment. I also took some summer courses so I was finished with my major in economics and completed my comprehensive exam and independent study requirements at the end of my junior year. By that time I only had one semester to complete before I was fully prepared to receive my degree.

During the summers in college I worked for three years as a chambermaid at the Molly Pitcher Inn. I really liked the job because of the people I worked with. There were the ladies who were full-time chambermaids and then the college students who were added to the staff during the summer months. The Molly Pitcher Inn in Red Bank, New Jersey, was an upscale hotel that featured fine dining and parking for boats on the river. We often had celebrities stay with us who were performing at venues mostly during the summer months since the hotel was on the Navesink River and only a few miles from the Atlantic Ocean. It was the premier hotel in our area in those days. I was assigned to work with an Italian lady, Maria, who hadn't been in the country for very long. She spoke reasonably good English and we became friends. I really liked her. The housekeeping manager was a wonderful woman. She must have had a strong connection to someone who had been mentally ill because she always offered work to those who had been recently released from our local mental hospital, Marlboro State Hospital, a psychiatric treatment center; and if these ladies had to return to the hospital for further treatment she held their jobs for them. I was very impressed by how she cared for these women who were former patients and tried to help them and her actions had a strong influence on me and my treatment of people who suffer from emotional or psychological illnesses. In fact I wrote a paper on the profound experience for one of my sociology courses. This experience had a tremendous effect on me and how I have viewed mental illness for my entire adult life and I have always been grateful that I found myself in this situation. I am sure this experience was impactful to me because of the struggles that I endured both in my past and also what I would face in my future. We still have a long way to go to truly understand and treat people who are mentally ill with proper care for them, but it certainly is a far cry from what people felt about mental illness and the mentally ill in the late 1960's.

We were also in school at a time when the social climate of college was changing dramatically. When I started at Wilson we had an older housemother who had an apartment in the dorm. She was there to guide us through the social aspects of college. I remember that we had a tea party every Sunday afternoon. I believe this is where my great love for all things tea started in my life. It was always well attended and lots of fun. We discussed issues of the day. We also had a curfew in the evenings and I think it was 11 p.m. on weekdays and 1 a.m. on weekends. Men were allowed in the dorm rooms from 1 p.m. to 4 p.m. on Sundays with the room door required to be open. By the time I graduated that all had changed. No more housemothers, no more curfews, and anything goes with the guys. Woodstock and all that. It all happened so fast it was like the last 25 years in our country squished into four years.

Dr. Martin Luther King Jr. was assassinated and shortly after that Robert Kennedy was assassinated. The world just seemed to come apart. And we understood but our parents for the most part had no idea what was happening. We marched and proclaimed our independence from their generation.

Along the way I was still really enjoying school. The level of intellectual development was so fascinating to me. I remember in my freshman English class we had to write a paper every week. It was a very content-driven school with so much reading and writing, and it had very high standards of performance. College was an enriching, happy experience for me.

However, at the same time, Ken was at the University of Maryland and would not be asked to return for his next semester because of his grades. It was the middle of the Vietnam War, and we really took a long hard look to figure out what he should do. He made the decision not to wait for the draft lottery and to sign up for a four-year hitch in the Air Force. He entered in February 1969, and on the day he finished boot camp they held the lottery and, as luck would have it, his number was 360, so he probably would not have been chosen but the decision had been made by us so it was useless to look back. This may have been the first time in my life that I realized the futility of looking back and wishing you could change the past. This was profound and life-changing to me and has served us well throughout our lives.

Ken was scheduled to complete all of his training in October 1969. My brother and I had travelled back to Guatemala in May of 1969, and Ken met us in New Orleans on the way to Guatemala. Ken and I became engaged in New Orleans. My brother brought the ring down with him as it was a family diamond. The diamond was not given to Ken for me; he had to pay $300 for it! Yes, another life lesson to be learned. Yes, I was ready to marry. I knew that Ken understood my very serious side and that he would not be able to tell me what to do with my life because of my strong personality, and we really, really loved each other and neither of us would ever want to go through life without the other one. Yes, I wanted my life to be of value on my own terms and nothing could change that, but to imagine life without him was absolutely impossible. For me, he was the one and that would never change. After five years of dating him I knew that he was a treasure and exactly the person that I needed in my life. God was so good to me to bring him into my life. He always laughs when I talk like this because he knows it is true and he thinks about all of the things I have done. He loved me just the way I was and he knew who I was and he was ready to accept me as I was. I felt the same way about him. I knew exactly who he was and we loved each other with no reservations.

Ken called me in early October 1969, the first semester of my junior year in college, and told me he was going to be stationed in San Vito, Italy. We had a decision to make. Would we get married at home on his leave or would I go over to Italy for the summer of

1970 to be with him and get married there, just the two of us? It would be quite something to put a wedding together in about three weeks. But we decided that we would much prefer to have the wedding in the United States with our friends and family with us. Well, I called my mother to tell her of our plans and she was close to hysteria when I told her. There was no way a wedding could be planned in that amount of time. "Oh yes, Mom, it can be done," I said. I had already spoken to the minister who would marry us, picked a date, set up counseling sessions with him which he required and ridden my bike to downtown Chambersburg to pick out a wedding dress, which I found with no problem. In addition I rode my bike to the hospital for the required blood tests. I had bought invitations that I could fill in with all of the necessary information, and got those started. My mother was able to firm up that the ladies of the church would be able to serve a luncheon in the fellowship hall for us. Ken had learned from his brother that we could borrow his car and reserved rooms to take a short honeymoon to Williamsburg, Virginia. My bridesmaid was a dear college friend (my freshman roommate) and the maid of honor was my best friend from high school. She was studying at Gettysburg College. Ken would drive us and my other college friends home to Fair Haven on the Friday before our Saturday wedding. I also picked out the maid of honor and bridesmaid dresses. Ken chose his brother as his best man and my brother and his friend from high school as ushers. My brother's best friend and lifelong friend from our neighborhood drove me and then Ken and me in his Cadillac on our wedding day.

There, it was all complete. There is a part of my personality that says I can do it if I just set my mind to it. I had even taken classes in the summer so that I could graduate in three and a half years. I couldn't believe that we were getting married! The only bad part was that he would be leaving for Italy the week before Thanksgiving and I would not see him again until May. But at least we would have a beautiful wedding with those who loved us and who we loved around us to celebrate the most wonderful day.

But it could not be that easy. My father refused to walk me down the aisle because he was suffering from Parkinson's disease. However, I took care of that by telling him that he *did not* have a choice, that I would hold him up, and he would be fine. I would not stand for that after he had failed me as a father and had not been supportive so many times in my life. This one time I insisted that he be a father to me. Like it or not he would do it.

I also had to listen to the whining and complaining of my mother as she was just beside herself and did not think she could handle the wedding with such short notice. Too bad, there is no choice; you will just have to muddle through. As an adult now I had some say in my life and the days of worry and unhappiness and drama that she loved would not take away from my happiness.

However, one last drama took place. As a young bride, one is always thinking about your new parents, your in-laws. They had prepared a lovely rehearsal dinner on Friday evening before the wedding. As we were leaving the church after the rehearsal my mother informed me that my parents would not be attending because they were "too tired" as usual and had to go right home to rest. Notice I did not say that she told my mother-in-law. I would have to deliver the news. Thank God these encounters would be few and far between now that I was no longer their responsibility. But, I sure was embarrassed by this ridiculous behavior, especially since the site of the rehearsal dinner was at Ken's family home only about one mile from my parent's house.

On the morning of the wedding I awoke and was so happy. I spent most of the morning in my granny's room just basically talking about life. My grandma and I had such a great relationship. Now that I am a grandmother I truly know what a special relationship it is and I treasure my grandchildren as much as my grandmother did hers. At one point my mother poked her head into the room and said, "What are you two talking about?" and we told her we were just talking. She said okay and went away. She had nothing to say to me. We chuckled about it and went on with our discussion.

We married in late October on a beautiful fall day with the sun shining and the leaves glistening in the sun with their beautiful fall colors and with a lovely breeze blowing. He was mine and I was his. We had no idea what the future had in store for us but I knew and he knew that whatever came our way we would handle it together.

After the wedding and the wedding night (the hotel where we spent our wedding night is still around and we drive by every once in a while) we drove back to school and on the way we dropped off our maid of honor at Gettysburg College. After all, we all still had classes to attend on Monday. As I said, we did sneak away to Williamsburg, Virginia, on Wednesday for a short time, returning on Sunday. He spent as much time as he could with me but then, all too soon, it was time to say goodbye.

You can't imagine how difficult it was for me to say goodbye to him knowing that I would not see Ken for six months. Six L-O-N-G months. But, somehow I made it, and I did well in my studies. During this separation, I even wrote an independent study which was well-received by the professors. I had an arduous schedule since I had two majors in sociology and economics and a minor in education. And during these six months I finished all of the work in my majors by the end of my junior year. By then I had a private room in a suite with a bathroom between. My suitemate went home for four days a week as her classes were only on Tuesday, Wednesday, and Thursday so it was very quiet and peaceful which helped.

I had been away from Ken for basic and his other training which was from February 1969 until October 1969, and then we were separated from November 1969 until May 1970, at which time I went to Italy to be with him. This was our first opportunity to spend some time together as a married couple since our wedding. I remember getting on the plane at JFK airport and flying to Frankfurt, Germany, where I stayed overnight and then on the Rome the next day and later that day, went onto the final leg of my air travel to Brindisi. We called the plane to Brindisi "The Brindisi Rocket" as it didn't have much time to get up and stay in the air before it was time to come down and land. Hence the name "rocket" because it was going quite fast and it felt like it was going straight up in the beginning of the flight and then straight down for the landing.

It was heavenly to be in his arms again and to feel the love between us. When we arrived at our apartment I met the neighbors and friends in our neighborhood. Everyone was so friendly and so happy to finally meet me. It was a wonderful welcome. Ken gave me a tour of the apartment, which he had rented and furnished all by himself. And when I say furnished I mean not only the furniture but also all of the linens and dishes and other items needed to run a home. He also purchased a car to prepare for my arrival. We had the night together and then, in the morning, he returned to work. Ken's particular job was on shift work. He worked four days from 4 p.m. to midnight, four days from midnight to 7 a.m., four days 7 a.m. to 4 p.m. and then he had four 24-hour days off. That would be interesting to adjust to, but as long he came home I didn't care. I was with him. He had done an awesome job preparing for my arrival, and to me everything was absolutely perfect.

But, more than just the shift work I had many things to adjust to. For example, the electric power frequently went off and we never knew for how long. We had a large water tank on the roof to service the four apartments in our building, so as soon as we knew that the power was off we would fill up our bathtubs for a backup supply of water. I also had a wringer washer at home which was an oddity but considered a treasure there.

That first day I was certainly trying to acclimate myself, and I decided to take a bath (no shower) and wash my hair. I had brought my hair dryer from the states and I plugged it into the transformer. I attached the hose to the bonnet and turned it on. It wasn't too long before I smelled something burning! It was my hairdryer; there were flames and smoke spewing out of the base. Oops, first casualty of the Italian electrical transformer. And, yes, I was using it properly, but the current fluctuated so much that it was a serious problem.

Laughter was the best medicine living there. At the time it was very primitive to us. For example we had one phone in our *town* at the local convenience store. I remember one of the first days on base someone asked me for my phone number, and I kept telling him that we had no phone. The man looked very confused and sort of scribbled over the telephone section of the form. Ken later informed me the telephone number was the phone number where he worked. We had no paved roads, no police that were assigned to our town and regularly lost power and water. Our gas stoves were powered by gas in a "bombola" or a container like a propane tank. When we needed a new tank the man came and detached the old one and put in the new one, after which he lit a match and moved it around the gas connection to make sure there were no leaks!

One day a friend and I went to the BX (Base Exchange) to buy groceries. She picked up a cake mix that we realized had a coupon on the back that had expired at least two years prior to the current date. We asked to see the manager who came over. She appeared to be a very haughty woman, and she went on to explain, "All of our food is inspected by the base veterinarian and as long as he says it is okay, it is fine to eat." Of course my response to her was "Woof! Woof!" Another time I remember washing clothes at the base Laundromat. A friend was with me. She had a little boy around two who had a fetish for silky material. He came around the corner with a woman's silk underpants on his index finger rubbing the inside of his ear. Ooh, wow! That woman was NOT amused but we sure had a good laugh after she left.

In spite of everything and all of the quirks we loved it there. We were together and in love and nothing was bad or inconvenient about that. We weren't even able to make a phone call home. We tried it once and it took more than four hours to connect. It was not worth it. So, here we all were, young people newly married and all alone relying on ourselves. As you can imagine it was difficult at times as we were just starting out, but we made so many wonderful friends, many of them we still see to this day. Most of the friends we made there were from Minnesota. One time when we were at Lake Mead near Las Vegas, my friend looked at me and said that I was the best friend that she had ever had in her life. It was true for me too, and it also sent me back to good old Specchiolla, which was the town that most of us lived in.

During that summer Ken told me that they might be sending him to Thailand flying in a C-130 airplane at tree-top level near the border with Vietnam. He was in the Security Service, or, as I called it, he was an electronic spy. I was not happy about this and decided to do something about it. I thought it would be a good idea to send letters to our senators in New Jersey. The first letters I sent came back to me. Hmm, was someone watching our mail? I then sent the two letters to my parents to mail for me. I did not keep copies of the letters. The basic premise of the letters was a long and well- thought out thesis on how expensive it was to send our servicemen to another post so often. I even calculated the costs. Then I included costs to move the families and the effect that it had on the children to move often and what a hardship it was for them. I don't remember the rest. Oh, did I mention that I did not tell Ken that I had sent the letters? One day two MPs came to our apartment after Ken's shift was over. They told him they were taking him to see the base commander but did not let on as to what it was all about. The commander wanted to talk to him about the congressional inquiry he had received. Ken was told by his commander that he did not appreciate receiving a letter saying that my letter to the senators had started a congressional inquiry. The letter the commander received needed to be answered within 24 hours. The commander wanted to know what my letter was all about and Ken was able to honestly say that he had no idea (which was why I did not tell him I had written the letters), and he didn't know what the base commander was talking about. The senators had found it worthwhile to investigate the contents of my letter and to turn the probe into a congressional inquiry. The base commander did not like the fact that he had to answer the inquiry in one day. Perhaps you can imagine Ken's face when he got back to our home. Remember that I said he accepted me as I am? Well that was exactly how he perceived the letter writing and he was proud of me for sure. It was quite something.

Years later I was watching a congressional inquiry on television and the senators were discussing ways to save money. During the discussion I noticed that everyone involved was drinking bottled water. I wrote a letter at that time saying that money could be saved in small ways and told them the Senate should go back to pitchers and glasses of water. The next time I turned in to see the Congress at work sure enough they were back to pitchers and glasses.

I had planned to go back to school in the fall but, with the possibility of Ken going to Thailand I decided to stay in Italy until January 1971. I was so happy to be with Ken it was amazing. We had so many friends and we travelled all over our area. The area has never been a tourist attraction per se, but we really enjoyed ourselves. We visited Bari many times and loved the beautiful cathedral of St. Nicholas. This cathedral was where St. Nicholas was entombed. He of course was the original Santa Claus and was born just three hundred years after Jesus was born. He had spent a great deal of his ministry caring for children's issues and had started the tradition of leaving gifts for children at their homes on Christmas. Bari also had a beautiful castle (really a fort). We also went to Alberabello and bought lots of bedspreads and blankets and even rugs. Alberabello is the home of the trulli houses that are round and have a spiral roof with no plaster or cement. The blocks are just placed in circles, each circle getting smaller and smaller until they come to a little pointed top. We visited Ostuni, the white city on the hill. It was there that we went to the church with the dead monks propped up in the basement. They were hung there when they died and they and their clothing just rotted over the years. The skin was dried on their bodies and their faces were quite distorted from the disintegration over time. It was an amazing sight to see. They were preserved for many, many years partially because of the climatic conditions of the basement since it was completely underground. When the skin had completely disintegrated the skulls were placed on shelves. It sounds creepy but it was just another place that was different from what we were used to here in the states.

We also visited Lecce and the beautiful pottery factory where the rows of finished Italian pottery went on forever.

We went to Rome many times. What an amazing city. Once we went to Rome when a very good friend of our friends was studying to be a priest at the American school in the Vatican. He was able to borrow a car and he took us to some of the out-of-the-way places that we had yet to see, including Castel Gondolfo, the pope's summer residence on a beautiful crater lake. Not only was he a wonderful guide but a great person as well. After we toured with him for the day he asked if we would like to come back to the school with him for a meal. What a treat. All of the meat that we had on base was from Yugoslavia, and it was tough enough to make soles for your shoes! But at the American College we had pot roast. We almost died it was so wonderful. We also enjoyed talking to the other residents of the school; they hadn't seen an American woman in a long time. After dinner they packed us sandwiches, drinks, and snacks for the train ride back to Brindisi.

The trains had compartments where you sat. The four of us had taken seats on one side of the car which left the other side vacant. An American woman poked her head in and asked if we had room for her and her family. We said of course and she and her two young daughters around eight and ten came in to join us. We chatted with them and found out that her husband was in the Navy and they were following the ship for the summer. The girls perked up when we got out our dinner and offered to share it with them. We had such a lovely time with them. A few days later we met the woman in downtown Brindisi. She called to us and told us that her husband was the captain of the ship and had wanted to have us come aboard for dinner at the captain's table. They tried to find us at the Air Force base but to no avail. However, we have never forgotten the wonderful gesture. She and her daughters were just people who needed some cheering up and we were glad to do it.

The weeks and months went by quickly, and it was again time to board the various planes that would return me to college. This was the most difficult thing that I had ever done in my life. I was leaving behind a husband who could not have loved me more and a place where I had so many friends – friends so different from any that I ever had before; and our little love nest of an apartment that was furnished with old, used furniture and a kitchen from the past. I cried my eyes out for days to the point where I was so spent that Ken worried whether or not I would be able to make the trip. But somehow I pulled myself together and said goodbye to him in mid-January 1971 and soon after found myself back at Wilson College. At least he would be there for my graduation in May 1971. The semester inched by with each day being longer than the one before. It was torture.

I remember receiving a very scary letter from Ken that described some bizarre incident that he assumed I knew about. About two weeks later I received a telegram from him telling me he had a frightening car accident. I remember hearing on the news that it had been snowing in Southern Italy (very, very rare), and during the storm a concrete truck came barreling towards Ken and the car turned around in a spin and hit a tree. His leg was badly bruised and he was shaken up. Our friend Bert had minor injuries and his hat had flown behind the back seat. Our poor car needed a new door but other than that was fine. It sure would have been better if I had received the telegram first before the letter.

The one upside to my final semester was that I had a suite that I shared with another student who went home each week from Thursday until Monday so I at least had some solitude while I was there. I never minded being alone. My senior year slowly and achingly ground to a halt and finally graduation was looming. Graduation was an extremely proud and glorious day for me. It had taken a horrible sacrifice to do the right thing and to leave Ken in Italy and return to college. I was very proud of myself and Ken. However, we were back together now and we were so in love and couldn't wait to get back to our beat up, old-as-the-hills furniture and our apartment with the beautiful view of the Adriatic Sea from our windows. Remember always that material things do not matter. If you have a place to live and a few pieces of furniture, great! In addition, if you have food to eat and clothes to wear, you have all you need. Money and things can never buy you or bring you happiness. Happiness and peace of mind are characteristics that you bring to yourself, and they are not influenced by things outside of ourselves. And to have love in your life is the most beautiful gift of all.

nine

Back Home to Italy

*F*inally we were on our way back to our own home to truly begin our lives together without any significant times of separation. And, along with our meager belongings, we had everything we needed. We left to go back to our home in Italy but of course there are always bumps (even small ones) along the way. After we got to the main airport in Rome, we switched to the local airport to take the "Brindisi Rocket" back home. Our flight to Rome was overnight but I was much too excited to sleep and Ken was also awake all night because I kept tickling him, blowing in his ear, poking him, and every other thing I could do to him to keep him awake. I just kept giggling and laughing. It was no use to try to ignore me or to reprimand me because I was just too happy to know that I had him all to myself for our forever, however long that would be.

When we got to Rome and went to the domestic airport, we discovered that our plane departure time had been changed from 9 a.m. to 7 p.m. We were so tired we decided to take turns sleeping so one of us could get some rest and the other one would take care of the luggage. Okay, I got to sleep first. When my hour was up Ken abruptly and rapidly woke me up and was asleep before I could sit up. This went on for several hours, and it was so funny each time we switched places. Boom, your time is up and I am now asleep. Life is just so much fun when you are with the one you love.

We got back to Brindisi and it was great to see everybody and meet the new people who had arrived. There were people from all over the United States, including Oklahoma, California, Pennsylvania, Iowa, West Virginia, Kansas, Illinois, Louisiana, and Minnesota. It was a wonderful experience for all of us and one that many of us never have. We learned so many lessons from our days in the service. I truly believe that being with others from all over the country whose lives and upbringing were so different from ours was a magical time and such a terrific learning experience. I wish all young people could have this time with others from around the country.

Unfortunately this is when the effect of my sexual abuse began to manifest itself in my adult years. The initial manifestation was that I began to suffer from severe panic attacks. I had no idea what was happening to me. I had them frequently enough for it to be extremely disturbing. The worst one I ever had was on a trip Ken and I took to Naples. As usual we took the train up north and got settled in our USO hotel. We got the tickets to go by bus to Pompeii the following day. That night we went to the NCO club to listen to a band concert. The Italian band was playing "Proud Mary" and we were laughing because they kept singing "rrrrrrolling on the "reeeever." Italians singing American pop songs just didn't sound the same. The next day we got up and got ready for the trip. We got on the bus. It was a beautiful day.

All of a sudden I began to feel ill as if I were going to pass out, and I was sweating profusely and felt sick to my stomach. I told Ken that I had to get off of the bus. I have never seen that look on his face before or since. Yes, I told him, you've got to tell the bus driver to stop and let us off. At first the bus driver looked perplexed, but he finally understood and pulled the bus over. We got off the bus and I sat down on the sidewalk near a drug store. Someone came out of the drug store and saw me there and went back inside to get the pharmacist who invited us into the store. I sat there for a while and they called us a cab. The ladies in the drugstore finally decided I was pregnant! They were so sweet. But, no, it was a full-blown and horrendous panic attack. When the cab came I slowly got in and the driver could see that I was not feeling well so all the way back to the hotel he kept turning around while he was driving and fanning me with his newspaper while both of us were thinking, "Oh my God, now we are going to be in a car accident."

We got back to the hotel and at dinner time Ken went out to find us something to eat. A gentleman in the street was following Ken asking him if he was looking for girls. Finally, Ken was so angry he told the man that he was out getting dinner for his sick wife. With that, the man smiled broadly and opened his jacket to reveal a great deal of jewelry and watches pinned to the inside and said to Ken "You want to buy a watch or perhaps some jewelry for your wife?"

The next day I was still feeling ill, and we decided to take the train home. Ken got me on the train and then got off to moisten a towel for me to use if I began to feel ill again. He was going to get the water from a water fountain near the train. The train was not supposed to leave for a while. However, as he was putting the towel into the fountain the train began to move. I screamed through the open window for him to get on the train, and when he whipped the towel from the fountain he splashed at least four people. The conductor who was waiting to get on the train ran up to him to tell him the train was not leaving yet. Now, while I was really freaked out by the entire experience in Naples, you can see why we would tell the story of our Naples trip over and over because laughter is truly the best medicine.

I had many other horrific panic attacks and never knew why. Once when we went to a party at a large hotel ballroom and someone was smoking a pipe I had a horrible attack. And another time I was also at a party and freaked out because a gentleman was playing the violin. Guess what, my father smoked a pipe and played the violin, but this did not occur to me until years later in therapy.

Still, there were so many good things about being away in Italy. You would think that the holidays would be difficult because we were away from home, but we all got together and brought food for each person. For example, for Christmas, the hostess made the turkey and someone else made a second one. We moved extra furniture from another apartment into the house so everyone had a seat. It never mattered how crowded it was. And the most important rule was that no single guys were ever left alone in the barracks. That was a must for me. Everyone added something important. One of the guys said grace, and someone made the gravy. All the vegetables anyone requested were on the table – baked potatoes, mashed potatoes, and sweet potatoes – and every possible dessert that anyone wanted. We wanted everyone to have their special taste of home. Someone else provided the entertainment with funny stories and memories of things we had done together. Also, the guys without children volunteered to work so we had to plan the festivities around work schedules and children's schedules but it always was wonderful. These celebrations were truly heartfelt expressions of love for each other and those around us. And they were simple expressions of the spirit we were celebrating and the wonderful people celebrating with us. And, again, these celebrations never revolved around money or things but always around people and love and happiness and the pure unadulterated joy of being together.

If we weren't enjoying the holidays, we enjoyed life in other ways – like watching the Italians fishing. They used two methods. For shallow water they would sprinkle bread crumbs and olive oil on the water and over the rocks, and when the fish came to eat the crumbs the fisherman would club the fish and pull them out of the water. The fish wouldn't be dead but just stunned. The other method was to go out in a rowboat, throw the nets out into the water along with a stick of dynamite, and, bam, when the dynamite exploded the stunned fish would fly into the nets and would be pulled into the boat.

We loved the beach. We had our favorite spot and went there when we could. Of course there were always others there, and our favorite thing to do beside swim was to drink Italian Spumante, the best bargain in Italy. We could buy three bottles for a mille which was about $1.60. It was absolutely wonderful, fresh and bubbly. To this day I still love Spumante.

There were no police in our town but we had Tony the Vigilante. He would come once a month and we would pay his fee. I believe it was one mille per month. Tony was always there when we needed him. He always followed the women when it was dark as we walked to a friend's house at night, when the guys were at work. You never knew that he was there. One of our friend's parents came to visit. His father went out to the car and Tony was right there with his rifle questioning why he was going into our friend's car. Once Tony realized it was Steve's father, everything was okay. Another time he saw that we had pulled over on the highway and he slowed down, and then turned around and stopped to ask us if we were all right. He was amazing.

One of the things that was difficult for all of us was the medical care. We did have a dispensary on base for urgent-care medical issues, but anything serious had to be treated in Germany. Emergencies were handled in the Italian hospital, but their medical care was very behind that in the US. Also, the language barrier made medical issues even more traumatic. If a woman was pregnant she had two choices for the delivery. She could either stay in Italy and have the baby at the local hospital or she could go to Germany to a very good American military hospital, but she had to go six weeks before the due date. If the baby was two weeks late the mother would be away for two and a half months from her husband and her children. If you stayed in Italy, you risked very archaic health care. A friend of ours went to the hospital for stomach pains and the doctor brought the x-ray to her and pointed to her IUD and asked what is was. He had never seen one before. Another friend went there to have a baby and ended up needing a Caesarean section. The nurse came in and made a vertical sign and a horizontal sign as her way to ask how she would want to be cut for the operation. There were many other incidents similar to this. It was always a difficult decision. We took care of three children who needed care when their mothers went away to Germany. We loved being with them at a time when they were separated from their mothers. It was a big responsibility to have children for such a long time but we enjoyed it.

We had wonderful friends who made the decision to have their baby in Italy. Unfortunately the baby had respiratory issues and was placed in an incubator with two other babies and one tube of oxygen stuck into the incubator. The baby was weak and basically just slowly passed away. I don't remember the hospital proactively doing much of anything to help or save the baby. We spent two weeks just constantly doing whatever we could to be helpful to them. It was the worst kind of torture. After the baby died they went home and then were stationed at a base in the United States. Our hearts broke for them, and I mean our entire community. We were a very close-knit family. It is one of the wonderful things about being in the service. And this experience was the very worst of them all. We saw our friend a few years ago, and he told us that when he retired he had set some money aside to put a headstone on his daughter's grave.

There was also a supper club on the base which was a lovely restaurant decorated in Italian décor with vines all over and olive oil bottles and wine bottles. It wasn't inexpensive and, since we hardly had any money left over at the end of the each week, it was only on rare occasions (or I should say very rare occasions) that we ate there.

One week we ran out of money and all we had to eat was peanut butter and jelly on very stale bread. It was certainly better than nothing. But my Granny sent us a letter with $5.00 in it so we could eat a good meal that evening. I usually made meals that could last a few nights such as beef stew, spaghetti and meatballs, or casseroles. I often made a tuna casserole with two tins of tuna that lasted for four nights. When we came home to the states Ken asked me never to make that again. I haven't.

We also had some festivals such as Oktoberfest and July Fourth. Everyone went to base and we all had a good time.

I never bought any clothes there for either of us and I bought one pair of boots at the market in Brindisi. But I never minded not having a lot of money to buy things. I was content and satisfied with my life. I was truly happy.

Then my parents expressed the wish that they would like to visit us and we said "Yes." We had an extra bedroom and were able to round up two single beds for them. American-made mattresses were made to be used on either side. But in Italy one side of the mattress was straw and the other side was padded. When I was making up the beds I didn't realize this and my mother's mattress was straw side up. Of course she complained bitterly and nastily, and it was then that we realized our mistake and flipped her mattress over!

We also had no central heat in our apartment. We had a large kerosene heater in the living room which heated that room, the dining room, and the kitchen. It was a real treasure since it meant we did not have to use the kerosene space heaters, which were tall and thin and very dangerous because the heaters were extremely hot. Many children were burned on them. We had one space heater which we let my parents use. One night after going to bed we heard them yelling for us. My father turned the control knob on the space heater the wrong way and the flames were leaping out and plumes of black smoke permeated the room. Ken quickly extinguished the flame, but there were smoke marks on the ceiling from the kerosene. We aired out the room and went to sleep. What a frightening moment that was and, in a way, in that moment, we passed from being their "children" to being their "parents." We had to assume their roles as they became almost childlike and we had matured into responsible adults after our time away from home. It was certainly an odd moment in time and one to be repeated on many occasions from that time forward.

By this time my father's Parkinson's disease had advanced and he was not walking well. We became tour guides and took them around to see the sights. I remember that while my father was there, I began to have regular and severe panic attacks again. It was awful to be so near him. We took them to many places in our area. It was so difficult to be around him and know that he was even staying under our roof. But I never would have turned them away and I survived.

And then something wonderful happened. The Vietnam War was winding down and Ken was offered an early out. He would separate from the service in June 1972 instead of February 1973. That may not sound like a lot but it meant that he could be back in the United States and could complete two additional semesters of college rather than if he arrived home in February. I went home with my parents to get somewhat set up before he returned home and I looked for a job.

ten

Back Home and in the USA

When Ken arrived home a few weeks later, we moved in with his parents. His mother had just had an operation and was bedridden for a while. Ken and his father went to work and I stayed home to take care of her. It was a terrific way to really get to know her and bond with her. It was a great experience. It is a fact that most times when a beloved son gets married, his mother is very anxious about his choice and spends time looking for flaws. No girl is good enough for my "perfect" son. Especially Ken!

At the time, my great aunt passed away and we were able to take any of her furniture that we wanted. We still have some pieces today. We got set up in a two-room apartment in Long Branch, New Jersey. He would be attending Monmouth College in Long Branch. I had a job as a part-time economics teacher and full-time substitute teacher at a local high school. I worked every day and really enjoyed it so much. I absolutely loved the kids and would do anything to help them.

At that time I realized that it is always wise when dealing with children to remember that they have NO way to change their lives. Adults must be their protectors and dream with them about their future. Sometimes the present is so difficult for children. Think about it; if something is happening to a child, he or she has no control over the situation. A child cannot move away from their family or change schools or move to a new neighborhood. The child's control of life is completely out of his or her hands. I am not saying this should change; but if you are listening to a child or trying to help a child, this certainly needs to be taken into account. Never, ever let a child you know feel powerless and alone. And remember, for example, if a child is being bullied, that it is not right. But chances are great that the bully is being mistreated and is acting out by finding someone who seems weaker than he is to feel power in his life. Children need to know this because it seems to help them cope and understand why it is happening.

One day while teaching I overheard a student saying that he had gotten a really good job and was going to move out of his house to live on his own. I had the newspaper with me and so I decided that it was a perfect time to teach the class a practical lesson about life and money. We looked up rents and figured rates for electric and heat and all of the other expenses. Then I looked at his paystub and told him what he was bringing home, which shocked him. He didn't realize there were taxes and other deductions taken out of his pay. It was a great lesson for all of them and they loved it and appreciated it.

I really enjoyed working with the kids and loved their spunk and enthusiasm. We always had a fun time in class, and I remember that I got a wonderful evaluation from my supervisor. As a substitute I also got to know so many of the kids. Many of the students in that district were children of servicemen as there was a large army base there, and many others were from low-income families. I always tried to make each child feel special and important. It gave me so much pleasure to help them in any way that I could.

I remember one evening Ken and I were walking down the street in town and a large group of kids was coming towards us. All of a sudden I was surrounded by them and they were patting me on the back saying, "Hey, Mrs. Aumack, how are you? What are you doing here?" Ken was off to the side wondering what was happening! But he could certainly see how much the children admired and respected me.

Once we took a school trip to Wall Street and the stock market. On the bus one of the kids lit up a joint, of all things. I just stood up and in a very loud voice said, "You've got to be kidding!" and that was that.

I did not want to stay as a part-time teacher and full-time substitute so I began to study my options. They were actually letting go one full-time social studies teacher where I was working. This was the time in the early 1970's when there were very few teaching jobs available and teachers were being furloughed in many districts. I sent out many resumes and had some great interviews, but there were no second interviews to be had. So I had no choice but to look elsewhere.

I had majored in economics so my next choice was business. I rewrote my resume and started to look in the want-ads and also went to many employment agencies. This was the beginning of the Equal Opportunity Act, and I was of course a big proponent of it. At one employment agency a young man was sent to one side of the office and I was sent to the other side. I asked why and was told that the left side was for the professional jobs and the right side was for the secretarial jobs. I left immediately as I would never be anyone's secretary with my education.

Finally I met with an agency that had a prospect for me with New Jersey Bell Telephone Company. The interview was in Newark, New Jersey, and I went there on the bus. I was having a very good day with no panic attacks. I went up there having no idea what the interview would be like. After I arrived I met with two gentlemen who explained the process to me. First, I would be given financial and other material which would be from a failing business and I would have to figure out how to save it. After I did that I would have to make a written recommendation of the steps that I would take to save the business. And finally I would give an oral presentation to the gentlemen to discuss my proposal. This was a long day to be sure, but I really enjoyed the process and felt confident about both my written and oral presentations. I felt strong and sure of myself. It took a few days for the letter to arrive but it was good news when it did. I got the job.

I called the employment agency and told them about the interview and how detailed and difficult it was. The representative said that he had been told the same by the others they had sent to the interview and added that none of the prospective employees had been hired. I told him that I had been hired and he was amazed and very pleased. So began the next chapter in my life.

After I was hired, I found out that the job I had applied for was that of a Customer Sales Representative at New Jersey Bell Telephone. Women were finally getting a chance to move into management positions, and I was the first woman outside of the company who had been hired for this position. My first business card showed my name as "S. J. Aumack" so that the customers would not know that I was a woman. The job entailed selling telephone equipment and services and making sure that the equipment arrived on time and was installed to the customers' satisfaction.

Before I could begin to work I had to be trained. The training was in Newark, New Jersey, and it would entail a month of study. That was when ferocious panic attacks set in, along with feelings of self-doubt. The training classes were difficult to endure. I tried to calm down and finally did feel a bit better after I got to know my classmates and the teachers, but as I look back it is difficult to believe that I could actually finish. Another time in life when I realized that I am a strong woman.

After the training course was complete I was ready to start in the job. The commute was about 30 minutes from our apartment. I was so panicked that my wonderful husband Ken and I stayed overnight in a hotel so I would only have to drive a mile or so to the office on my first day at the job. Being with my husband – my rock – meant everything to me. I was determined to succeed after having been given such a wonderful opportunity, and he was equally determined to be there for me and with me.

I survived that first day and thrived at the job. This was the beginning of competitive telephone equipment and I was very successful in fighting the competition. I was assigned a male partner. We handled all the cases from our office where the customer revealed any interest in buying equipment from another company. As this was at a time before computers were used for presentations, I used a flip chart which I made up using brochures from the company to reference all of the products. The flip chart was very successful and was eventually reproduced and used by all of the sales representatives in the company. During this time our team of two had a 93% win record, and we received many letters of praise from clients and accolades from the company. One of my favorites was an article in the company newspaper that talked about my success in the business. The article quoted me as saying, "The actual installation of the customer's equipment went very smoothly and efficiently with no interruption of service." The article went on to say that the customer was so pleased with Shirley's interest in the quality of his telephone service that he sent a letter to New Jersey Bell Telephone expressing his satisfaction with the manner in which she handled his service relocation. "Mrs. Aumack demonstrated a fine grasp of our communications needs and saw that they were scrupulously met. Mrs. Aumack deserves recognition for her own capabilities and intentions in assuring our uninterrupted service." I was in my element and felt empowered as I had in college.

I was also very outspoken. The men whom I worked with could not believe how I would talk to the bosses and tell them exactly how I felt, rather than the "politically correct" company line. They told me that the reason I did that was because I was married and my husband had a job. I did not have to be afraid of losing my job. Actually, that was my true personality.

One day my boss told me all about his beautiful boat and he asked me if I would like to accompany him on it. I told him that my husband and I love boating and would love to go out with him. That subject never came up again. I learned that I had a natural ability to make my point very clearly without being nasty or frightened.

Another thing I learned was that I liked working with men. We got along very well and I fit in with them. My partner in the competition unit was a very confident guy. He clearly thought he was a strong and qualified guy. He was someone who could look down on people.

In spite of this we worked very well together and never had any problems with our joint assignments. Our personalities were so different that we complemented each other. I was also in a carpool with two of the men in the office. A group of us really became close friends and we socialized together, as well.

I remember the time when I was being evaluated in the field by my manager, and he said that he would like to give the presentation to the customer. I was happy to let him present our message. During the presentation the customer kept looking at me like, *"What is he talking about?"* and I had to make my presentation after the manager was finished. The entire visit ended on a high note as the customer was very satisfied with my discussion with him, and all was well. When I got back to the office the guys asked me how the "evaluation" went. I told them what had happened and they asked me how the manager did with the presentation. My answer to them was, "Well, he couldn't sell a bone to a dog!" We all had a good laugh over that.

Another time a group of us, who used to stay after work to talk to each other, were reported to the management for staying after work and asking for overtime pay when we were really just shooting the breeze. We were called into the boss's office and politely told not to do that. While we were eligible for overtime if we stayed after hours, we never put in for the time unless we were doing work. I asked for the name of the person who reported us and of course the manager would not give me the name, but I figured out who it was and confronted him. I directly asked him if he had reported us and he was surprised by that, but, he did answer that, yes he had. I explained, without any anger, that we were not asking for overtime pay for the times we were just socially discussing things. No fuss, no bother, just a nice conversation with one of the senior reps.

I learned so much in this position, including how to deal with people, both the customers and other reps as well as all of the people whom I worked with. I really can't find the words to describe what this experience meant to me. My confidence soared and it was an experience that was as important in my life as college. I loved it.

I was there for about three years when Ken decided he would start looking for a new job. He found one in Massachusetts and we began the process of moving.

The telephone company did everything they could to find me a job there. I received a letter from the head of human resources in Massachusetts who told me she felt as if she knew me personally. She had received so many calls and letters letting her know that she should find a place for me! But I had another job waiting for me...

eleven

Our Children

I was pregnant! We had been married for eight years at that time, and I had lost a baby earlier when we lived in Italy so we made the decision that I would not pursue a job during this precious time for us. The pregnancy was somewhat difficult for me. I was very dizzy at times and was not able to drive for several months. There were issues with the baby as well. I understand very little about medical issues and have always chosen the best physicians I could, so I didn't need to worry if they told me not to worry. The baby showed a blood irregularity and I had to have blood tests that were sent weekly to a special laboratory in California. At the time of the pregnancy I weighed about 135 pounds. I began to gain weight a little too fast for the doctor, and I remember that I tried to watch my weight. I never had an issue with my weight, I believe mostly because of my high nervous energy. But now I was very happy and relaxed. It really irked me that I had a weight problem. I tried very hard not to gain too much weight, and I think I gained about 30 pounds. After every doctor weigh-in I went right out and bought some sinful food like a cheesecake. The pregnancy proceeded with no problems other than the ones mentioned above and soon it was time to have the baby.

My labor was very slow and I ended up in labor for seventeen hours and had to be medicated to speed up my labor. Then, before the delivery, I was encouraged to have an epidural to numb the pain. Our son was born healthy and absolutely beautiful. However, when I think back on the birth I remember three things…that before the birth the doctor sat at the end of the bed and squatted down and leaned over to see how the labor was progressing and his toupee, which was attached in the front, fell over his face. My goodness, I can't believe we didn't burst out laughing. The second thing that I always remember is that I swore I would never have another epidural. The process of the epidural was not one I would care to repeat as the birth process was shorter than the process to have the epidural. Lastly, before Ken left that evening, after I had the baby, I asked him to bring me a dozen Dunkin Donuts. He did bring them the next morning on his way to work, and when he came back to the hospital after work I had eaten the entire dozen. So there. I also remember that the law had not been passed in the country to require health insurance companies to pay for pregnancy and birth. That was a lesson well learned and taught me to always look into every nook and cranny before making decisions in life that affect your finances. And so, we didn't "own" our little son for quite a few months. Of course very soon after, the law requiring health insurance companies to cover routine pregnancy and delivery was passed.

We took him home. He was amazing and a great baby. We loved almost every moment of parenthood. I remember being for the most part a very relaxed mother who really enjoyed having a child. I breast fed him for more than eighteen months. One of our fun memories with our son was when we introduced him to the house we had bought just after he was born. We put him on the kitchen table in his baby seat and his eyes nearly bugged out when he looked at the kitchen wallpaper. It had very large with very bright yellow, orange, and brown sunflowers. He was a wonderful baby and toddler and brought great lightness, laughter, and joy into our lives.

Just about the time we were thinking about a second child, I discovered that I was pregnant again. Our second son was born about two years after our first child. I changed to a doctor that did not believe in medication during the birthing of the baby. He would only provide medication if the patient asked for it. During the birth the baby's heartbeat fell dramatically and I had to be rushed into the delivery room with oxygen. During the transport the tube fell off the oxygen tank. I kept trying to get Ken to let go of the mask so I could tell him that the tube was not working and I could not breathe. Finally a nurse who was pushing the gurney realized what was happening and she re-attached the oxygen tube. At last, I was able to breathe. Our second little son was born very quickly and I watched as the cord was unwrapped four times from around his neck. After the birth, the doctor and Ken and I prayed for him to be okay. Our pediatrician examined him and told us he was fine. He had a full head of dark brown hair when he was born and was a very chunky baby, weighing in at almost nine pounds.

I had a much easier pregnancy the second time, and my biggest worry was how I would be able to handle two children. I prayed about it for a while and then I realized that many people had survived with two children and I would surely be able to handle it. And I was correct!

By this time, I had thoroughly immersed myself into our community. I had called to find out if there was a "Newcomer's Club" in town. I was given the name of the woman in charge of the club, and she was just attempting to organize a new group to reestablish the club to active status. I went to the meeting and of course volunteered to be the president. I met several other women who were interested in being officers, and from there we started to re-activate the Wilmington Newcomers Club. It was a success from the start, and by the time our family moved back to New Jersey two years later the group had grown to number 30-plus women. We had evening socials, afternoon play time with the children, and co-ed nights out with our husbands. It was a great group and I enjoyed playing the part I did in its success. We met many wonderful folks and have great memories of our times together.

During this time I had told Ken that I really wanted to get some type of part-time job as I missed working. As luck would have it, I read an ad in the paper from H&R Block that they were offering a tax course and looking for tax preparers who could work after completion of the course. I packed the kids in the car and we drove to the H&R Block office where I could sign up for the course. I remember it like it was yesterday. I went in and asked the person at the desk if this was where I could sign up for the course. She said yes. I then asked if I needed to take a test to sign up for the course and she said no. I gave her my check for the course and she gave me the information concerning the class locations and I signed up for one nearest to me in the evenings. When I left the office with the boys, I was overcome with emotion and cried feeling like I would finally be able to re-enter the adult world. I also remember how happy I was to have a husband who would take over the responsibility of the boys for two nights a week while I was at the course. He was a real peach. The course was very practical and somewhat difficult and certainly time-consuming as it came with a great deal of reading and homework. But I really loved the work and being able to use my brain power again. One thing I do remember about the evening course was trying to stay awake during the class. I worked for H&R Block in Massachusetts for one tax season nights and weekends and I loved it. I enjoyed the work and I enjoyed working with the public.

At this time Ken had decided that his job was going nowhere fast. He had been told that he was hired to replace the manager who was in charge of his department. However the man never retired and Ken was getting anxious to get on with his career. We discussed where he should look for a new job and decided that we would not want to move to a new place again so it would be either Massachusetts or back to New Jersey.

It wasn't long before he found a job in New York City. We were off on a new adventure with our goal of moving back to the county in New Jersey where we had met in high school. Ken started working relatively quickly after being hired in his new position. He was living in New Jersey during the week at my parent's house because it was closer to the train station. He would come back to Massachusetts on the weekends. I stayed at our Massachusetts house with the children. I needed to keep the house neat and clean because we were selling it, and, of course, and I had all of the responsibilities with the children during the week. And the packing needed to be done as well. As always Ken helped as much as he could in his usual helpful way as he could each weekend. We did not like to be separated so it was difficult to say goodbye each Sunday.

Fortunately, the realtors almost always called me before coming. The boys and I were there for three months before we moved to New Jersey. We had not looked at homes as we thought it would be better to have the house in Massachusetts sold and closed before buying another house in New Jersey.

At that time we returned to New Jersey and lived with Ken's parents. Their house had three extra bedrooms so we had plenty of room. The children were well behaved and all went well. Ken's parents really enjoyed their grandchildren as they were lots of fun. They were almost always happy and smiling.

Soon we found a lovely home with a great yard for the children and moved in. There were many young families in the neighborhood so the children were able to make friends and so were we! We settled in and for the most part we were happy to be home again in New Jersey.

The children grew and were doing well. We enrolled them in preschool and I continued to take classes and work at H&R Block in New Jersey. Before my fourth season working at H&R Block, I decided to teach the basic income tax class in the fall. It was there that I met a woman who was taking the course, and she engaged me in conversation about starting a new business with her as a partner.

After a great deal of thought and discussions with Ken, I decided to accept her offer. It was a great opportunity. One thing I will never forget is that I did call a few of my H&R Block clients and told them that I was moving into my own practice. All of them came with me and became financial planning clients as well, and they and their children were with me until I retired on December 31, 2013.

This was also the beginning of my career as a financial advisor. I had thought a great deal about the next steps in my career. I had thought very seriously about becoming a Certified Public Accountant but after much soul searching I realized that what I loved mostly about preparing income taxes was the interaction with the clients. I loved working with people, even the difficult ones, and helping them to the best outcome on their income tax returns. Most Certified Public Accountants concentrate on the numbers and not on the people! Financial planning was a relatively new profession and seemed to be made for someone like me. I had a terrific grasp of the numbers and loved to show people the best ways to use their money to receive the best results for them in their own circumstances.

But, wow, there was so much to learn about the profession and so many licenses and designations to earn to be a true professional in the field. I remember that for many years I would go upstairs after dinner to our bedroom and study for all of the various licenses that I needed to become a qualified financial advisor. First of all was my life insurance license, and after that my securities license, and then I took on the Internal Revenue Service exam to be classified as an enrolled agent. That one was very difficult because I had to pass a sixteen-hour exam given over two days. The Certified Financial Planner designation at that time required the completion of six courses with an exam after each course. In the evenings while I studied Ken took care of the children and got them ready for bed. I was so fortunate to have a real partner to help me with the work that I took on to further my education and become a true professional. It took me several years to get all the licenses and designations.

At that time I worked hours that coincided with my children's school schedules so I was able to be a mom as well. As the practice grew I did use a babysitter during tax season for two seasons so I could extend my day to accommodate my clients. At that time the office was very close to our home and so I was able to be home when the children came home from school and to spend time with them and cook dinner for the family, and then the babysitter took over around

6 p.m. until Ken arrived home from New York City around 7 p.m. It was a crazy schedule during tax season. As the business grew and I was much busier, I used to work until 9 or 10 p.m., which made it difficult to sleep! As you can imagine it was a trying time for me but I really loved every minute of it! I was a successful business woman, a good and present mother, and a happy wife. Life was good.

Ken and I really enjoyed being parents. We truly loved our children and used every possible opportunity to be with them and enjoy family life. We all loved music and did a lot of singing and dancing in the evenings. After dinner we usually spent time together watching "The Muppet Show" and we also did a great deal of reading to the children. We also started travelling when they were four and six years old. I remember our first trip was to Mystic, Connecticut. It was there that we realized our oldest son had a great love of history. Our youngest was not the best traveler and he asked over and over again "Are we there yet?" As soon as we got there he cried and told us he wanted to go home. Fortunately we bought him a seagull on an elastic band and he bounced the bird up and down for the remainder of the trip and was happy.

I remember our second son learned to talk much earlier than our first son. And he spoke so well that many people used to comment on his verbal skills and would ask me what his first words were. I always answered, "Pardon me, do you have any Grey Poupon?" which always elicited lots of laughter. He was also very inquisitive and asked me questions all day long. Some days it was just too much and I would answer, "I am sorry but you have used up your quota of questions for the day." He would have an odd look on his face and go back to playing. Sometimes he would say "Why can't I ask any more questions?" I would just add that I was sorry but that was a question.

I always made a point not to criticize the children. For example, I didn't say to my son, "Stop asking me questions; you are driving me crazy!" I always found a way to quietly get them to understand without any drama. Another unusual way I had to discipline them was with an empty two-liter soda bottle. If they were fighting I would bop them on the head with the plastic bottle, which got their attention and they knew what that meant. Stop fighting. Always quiet with no yelling.

My mother was not a yeller, but she always had a way to make you feel small with her comments, criticisms, and observations. She was critical about anything and everything. I hated that and refused to do that to my children. I wanted a peaceful home, and I wanted them to grow up knowing that they were wonderful people and that their mistakes could be discussed quietly and with respect. Always look at the good in people, especially your children.

The boys loved to play dress up and we soon had many "costumes" around the house. They would be cowboys, Mexicans with big sombrero hats, dress up like motor cycle cops (CHIPS) taken from a television show of the same name, spies like us following the movie of the same name, and popular duos such as Batman and Robin. They spent many hours outside playing happily in all kinds of weather.

Our youngest loved to eat, and we had many calls to poison control as he would eat berries in the yard and other tempting flora and fauna. An older neighbor told us the children would enjoy watching the birds pick on a chicken carcass so we put one in the yard only to see our youngest picking the chicken off of the bones. I even had to keep the kitchen garbage can hidden as I would find him rummaging in it looking for food.

Our oldest didn't like to eat at all. I learned many tricks to help him try food and to eat enough to sustain him. I had the two-out-of-three rule, which meant at dinner he had to finish at least two of the items on his plate. I also told him that all meat was steak which he liked to eat. He was also very excitable and would not eat when we went to other people's homes, so I learned to feed him at home so at least I knew he had something in his stomach before we went out for dinner at friends and family.

Then came the next huge decision and change in our lives. We decided to move again. We had been unhappy with the school system in several ways, and we also loved where we both lived when we graduated from high school. Ken had lived there and gone to school there for his entire life. I had moved there when I was a sophomore in high school. Again in our lives we were on the same page and it meant so much to us. The public school the children were attending was fine, but we wanted more for our children. We started looking at private schools and found one right in the same area where Ken and I had gone to public school. Back in 1989 this private school would have cost us $10,000 a year, which seemed like a great deal of money, not to mention that it would have been a great inconvenience to drive there since the school was about fifteen miles from where we lived. So Ken and I put our heads together and realized that it would be better to move all of us to the town with the better school system where they could both walk to school. As luck would have it, I visited the local elementary school and the secretary to the principal had graduated from high school with me, which I took as another good omen. Also, the secretary to the superintendent had gone to school with Ken since kindergarten. They were both friends and lovely and warm people and made us feel even more comfortable with this major decision.

In addition to this I had had serious issues with my business partner and I was contemplating moving on. Although this was secondary to the children's issues, things had become seriously broken between us in many ways. I was very unhappy about the way she treated many of our clients. She would discuss clients with other clients who knew each other and sometimes were related. It was incredibly inappropriate and completely unprofessional that she shared personal information that should have stayed confidential. As time went on I discovered with no surprise that she had said many inappropriate things about me, as well. She was very insecure, and to compensate for that she felt she had to show people how great she was. It was not my way at all. She took several clients to court over non-payment issues. She lost each case but had her day in court and stated her case and, of course, was always outraged when she lost. In one case a woman came in to see her to discuss how she should invest her money. My partner spent some time with her client going over her options and, when the client decided on a course of action different than my partner recommended, my partner billed for her time. Payment for her time was never discussed so the woman rightly refused to pay the bill. The judge ruled on the side of the client, as I knew he would. This happened more than once and it irritated me each time. I also knew that she was cheating me out of money that she owed me from the tax business. I suspected it all along the last year I worked with her and it was confirmed to me by the bookkeeper.

Another very irritating trait she had was to always blame the client when a mistake was made. It was never her fault or the company's fault if there was any kind of mistake. She would spend hours trying to figure out a way to blame a client, for example, if a mistake was discovered by the client or the Internal Revenue Service on a tax return. Everyone at the office would be involved in trying to find a way to blame the client. It was ridiculous. I remember the first time I made a mistake on someone's tax return when I had my own office. After the clients called me I looked at the return and my notes and paperwork and found where I had made the mistake and called the clients back. I told them that they were right and I was sorry. Do you know what they said? "Oh, that's alright, we all make mistakes!" And they said that I should just fix the error and everything would be fine. Okay! It felt so good to NOT waste all of the time we used to waste! And it was much better to just admit my mistake! And the clients were fine with it! There are not many mistakes in life that cannot be corrected.

And so, wanting to move our children to a town with a better school system, we put our house on the market and sold it rather quickly. Our new home and lot were similar in size and we were able to adjust to our new surroundings without too much trouble. And we soon found out that many of the people with whom we had gone to school had the same idea and also came back to live in the same area.

We moved in the fall of 1989 when the boys were ten and twelve. There was a great deal to do in order to get the boys settled into school. I had problems getting our youngest son into the proper classes because, even though he had wonderful grades, the new school did not think his grades would be equal to the same level of excellence in the new school. It took me a while to make sure that both of them were properly placed in the correct classes based on their abilities, but I was able to do so. Ken and I were satisfied that the hard work I had done to see that the children were properly placed was successful. Our way of handling our children was so different from the inept way my brother and I were handled by my parents.

On a side note, I have something to say about seeing that your children have all that they need to succeed in school. I remember attending a meeting with Ken of parents of children who were in the child study group environment. The people involved gave a beautiful presentation of what they did and how they tried to help the children meet their full potential. After they had finished they asked if there were any questions from the audience. Lots and lots of hands went up. What did these parents want to know? *Why is my child getting extra help? My child doesn't need this! How do I get them out of this program?* Here I was in the audience so happy that my son was getting what he needed and remembering that I had to move to get the help that he needed. And we didn't have to pay for it since our taxes were paying for it! I couldn't believe the people in the audience. So, if your child needs help and gets it, remember that this is a very special gift and is never something to be ashamed about.

The children continued in that school system until they graduated from high school. Through the years we helped them get into activities that they loved. They were both immersed in the music programs in elementary school and high school. They both played in the marching band in high school. They also participated in the drama program at the high school and were in almost every production during their years in high school. I remember as President of the Performing Arts Society, I always gave a talk to the parents during the PTA school open house about the performing arts activities in the school. But I also made it very clear how important it was to see that their children got involved in activities in high school as it helped them in many ways and definitely kept them out of trouble. At that time many parents thanked me for my remarks and how I had made them understand at a deeper level how important it was for children to be in activities while in school. Not to mention that it kept them out of trouble! In fact, I didn't want to force my children into after-school activities so I used a little psychology on them. I told them that the television could not be turned on until 8 p.m. at home so that they would be looking for things to do. When they complained about how bored they were, I went over all of the after-school activities that were available to them to help alleviate their boredom. This is how they became so active in after-school activities. They had so much fun and made wonderful friends who were also engaged in the activities the boys enjoyed.

We also had a great family life. When the children were young an older couple told us that their grown children always told them that all of their vacations had meant so much to them and I never forgot that. We went on so many trips through the years. Our first trip was to Mystic, Connecticut, and we believe that is where our oldest began to really become interested in history. As the trips came and went, our youngest showed his interest in science. Many times when we travelled we went to historical sites and science museums so each would use the vacations to build interest in their lifetime passions. We travelled to many lakes, which were always a favorite of mine, such as the New Hampshire lakes, Lake Champlain, Lake Oswego where we also saw the Baseball Hall of Fame, and lakes in the Adirondacks where we also did quite a bit of fishing. We took day trips one year to landmarks around us in New York City, Philadelphia, and New Jersey. We travelled out west to the Badlands; Mt. Rushmore; Fargo, North Dakota; Denver, Colorado; and a rodeo in Cheyenne, Wyoming. We went to California and Tijuana, Mexico, and many other places. When our oldest got older we toured many Civil War sites. And we never gave up on those science museums either. We had so much fun wherever we went. Ken loved to travel and it was not unusual for him to get us out of bed at 7 a.m. to start the day and to return to our hotel at 11 p.m. The days were long and crammed with fun. The children always tried to pick out music that would irritate Dad just for fun and we would all sing along to the music. Sometimes they would even tell Dad, "Oh please, not another scenic outlook, Dad! We are just not getting out of the car!" Once in North Carolina a waitress said to us, "I see many families travel through here, but I don't think I have ever seen a family having so much fun!"

Along the way we tried to teach them what I always called "life lessons" in our own unique style, with no criticism of them or yelling at them. For example, when they were around eight and ten and I was driving them somewhere, one of them opened the window and threw out a candy wrapper. I pulled over to the side of the road and they asked why I was stopping. I told them we had to get out of the car and go back and find the wrapper. They wanted to know why since others had thrown paper along the road. I explained to them that we did not do that. It was a busy road and they were somewhat frightened as we walked down the street to find the particular wrapper they had thrown away. We did find it, scurried back to the car and were on our way. That was the first and last time they ever did that.

Another lesson I wanted to teach them was to always open the door for a women. I started teaching them to open the door for me and one day I decided it was time for a test. We were at the mall and they forgot to open the door for me so I just waited outside the mall for them to realize I was not with them. They walked through the store and when they got to the entrance of the mall they turned around and walked back to the door wondering where I was. When they saw me patiently waiting for them outside the door they came out and said, "What's wrong, Mom?" I said, "Nothing. I am just waiting here for you to open the door for me." They never forgot that also. No yelling or pointing fingers, we just went off to complete our shopping.

Another trip that we took that was also a favorite was our trip to Florida to a Penn State bowl game. Since there were four of us, we decided to make different shirts, one with each word of a favorite Penn State cheer, *We Are Penn State*. As head of the family Ken wore the "We" shirt, I was "Are," our Penn State son's shirt was "Penn" and our other son was "State." As we were walking to the dining room, the boys were ahead of us and we noticed that they had held the door open for an older couple. The couple waited for us and asked us how we had taught them to be so polite. I was able to share the story about the mall door and we all had a good laugh together. As we entered the dining room at the hotel, everyone was commenting and pointing to our shirts. Ken had stopped to go to the bathroom and someone called out "Hey, where is 'We'?" I laughed and said. "'We' is going WeeWee!" And when "We" entered the room everyone pointed, clapped, and cheered!

Both of the boys grew into wonderful young men who made us extremely proud. They both had learned through us and from us how to treat others and how they should be treated. They had a father who was a wonderful example of how a man should act in the world. And they had a mother who had been terribly abused but had not become an abusive parent and did everything she could to protect them and care for them.

They both went on to college and did very well in their studies. Our oldest spent most of his college years in New York City. I remember waking up every morning to see sights of New York City on the news and thinking how amazing it was that my eighteen-year-old was living there. But Ken also worked in the city and had given him lots of clues on how to behave there. One was to look in the windows of the buildings to see if anyone was following him. One time he thought someone was following and he decided to act weirdly and the person crossed the street to get away from him. But he loved the city and took full advantage of everything he could as a student while he was there.

Our youngest son who was more of an introvert went to school in Pennsylvania and was in an environment as far away from the city as possible. I can remember that we used to look for things to talk to him about and we started watching "American Idol" so we could talk about it with him when we called him. When he first went to school he would call us after each football game to talk to us about it. The first time he did not call us after a game made us so happy because we knew that he was making friends. In addition to earning their

Bachelor's degrees, they each have their Master's degree in their field of study. Today they are successful members of society of whom we can be very proud.

What a dichotomy this is from my relationship with my own parents. I really never felt close to them, and I can't say that there were many times in my adult life that I enjoyed being with them. As a child we did go on great vacations to New Hampshire and the Jersey shore, but it was the times I spent with my brother and cousins that were fun for me. I could never say it was fun to travel with my parents. They always complained about every little thing.

Our family life was so different and so much fun. We enjoyed being together as a family and took advantage of every opportunity to be a family.

twelve

My Personal Therapy

When you walk through a storm…
Survivors typically go to therapy to find out what is wrong with **them**, not what was **done** wrong **to** them.

I was in individual and group therapy for nine years of my life. The therapy for me started when I called a male therapist I had known of and asked him if I could meet with him to discuss my lifetime of insecurities and panic. You may also remember that I was much more comfortable working with men, which also influenced my decision to see a man. I firmly believe that it was because of how ineffective my mother was in her capacity as a mother. In the beginning of the therapy I was just searching for the reasons that I could be so strong in one moment and so scared and intimidated in the next. Little did I know that I was on a long journey that would take everything that I had to complete it.

Therapy was absolutely gut-wrenching. It was awful. It was very, very painful because I fought it every step of the way. I treated my therapist as the evil villain in my life, just waiting for him to hurt me, to make fun of me, or to bring me back to the place where I was in my childhood bedroom in the dark with my father. It was so difficult for me to be vulnerable in therapy. I could not let down my strongly erected defenses and be honest about myself. These feelings of complete insecurity did come up to the surface fairly frequently but I could not express them. And I had to express them as that was how I would face all of my past and would be able to become a healthy adult.

Having very little knowledge of the therapy process and, at that time, not really knowing what I would discover about my past, feeling uncomfortable there was certainly to be expected. In the core of my being, however, I felt so strongly that something was wrong with me. I also thought that maybe he wanted to have sex with me and I was never sure why I felt this way. For some reason that did not upset me. He certainly in no way ever acted this out. It was the most uncomfortable time in my life, bar none, except of course for the years when I endured my father's sexual abuse. When I was there with the therapist I felt protected, and after I left I couldn't wait to go back there again. I felt both pain and disgust while I was with the therapist, but I also felt protected in that room. Again, as I said in the beginning of this chapter, I felt there was something wrong with me, that I was a horrible person, not that something had been done wrong to me. It was so excruciatingly painful and horrible to discuss my childhood with him that it took me at least two years before I could even admit to being sexually abused by my father. His patience was beyond human parallel.

I have pages and pages of transcripts of telephone messages from him and many, many letters that I wrote to him. I have no idea how he had the patience to work with me. I remember once, far into our relationship, that I had asked him if I was the most difficult case he had ever dealt with; and he said the only one that was as difficult or possibly worse was a woman who was a survivor of the Holocaust. I'm not sure how I felt about that! I knew that my suffering was fierce and my deepest perception of myself was that I was the lowest of the low, worthless at every level. And, of course, as my father had told me with certainty, that nobody would ever help me and nobody would ever love me.

My father had been essentially out of my life since the day I left for college in that I never cared or thought about what he thought of me and my life choices. And Ken despised my father in the same way that my grandmother despised him. But not allowing my father to be present in my life did not change what he had done to me.

I started therapy because I had come to the point in my life where I was not comfortable in my own skin and could not take it anymore. There was something WRONG but what was it? I finally understood that my anxiety did not stand alone but was a sign of something deeper. In the whole of my being and at the base of my self-worth and self-esteem, I also always felt so unworthy and never taken seriously. I remember in snippets the moments in my life when I would be sailing along feeling so good about myself and strong and in control and then, because of a word, a smell, a sound, a look, a sneer, a sight, a taste, or a touch, how I would be catapulted outside of myself from the present back into the dark, twisted, horrifying space where I was spinning completely and totally out of control. It happened anywhere, anytime, in any circumstances, under every possible condition in my life. These swirling, wrenching, hurtling, horrifying journeys would take place in an instant and happen anywhere…on the couch in my living room, boarding a bus and feeling there was no escape, watching little children playing in the park, while screaming at my own children for no reason, singing a favorite song, walking into a room and seeing or sensing something, being overcome by a smell or a taste or a sound, in a waiting room, listening to music on the radio. Something was there but what? What made me so strong one moment and so vulnerable the next? I just had to know…

I knew that some of this was because of my mother's inability to mother me. My mother was an intelligent woman who, as I mentioned earlier, had skipped one year of high school. She finished high school in three years which is quite an accomplishment. After that she attended secretarial school and had gotten a good job at the Prudential Insurance Company. She did have friends throughout her life who liked her very much and she had a good social life. Some of her earlier friends were friends for her entire life, and she easily made friends throughout her life. Most of these people would never have guessed what a terrible mother she was.

In spite of her social life she was very naïve about life and what was and is important and unable to truly mother her children. She was someone who had very poor coping skills. Between my mother and my father, the two of them had the coping skills of one-half of an adult. She was not able to handle her problems, and incapable of handling those of her children. She made no attempt to help us handle our problems. When we came to her with a problem in our lives, she reacted like these issues were way beyond what she could handle. She seemed to have no confidence in herself as a mother and exhibited very weak coping skills to us. This made her unable to guide us through the simple issues of everyday life in general or to deal with any of our specific emotional needs. She was very negative about life overall and about her situation in life in particular. For example, when a problem came up for either my brother or me, she could not sit with us and reason about how to deal with the issue. An example of this is how I lost interest in playing the piano. As a mother she never questioned why I wanted to stop playing. My piano teacher told my parents that I was very talented, and she could tell that I loved music and the teacher was very upset when I seemed to lose interest in playing. She talked to my parents and said that something had happened and that I had lost my love for the piano and that she wouldn't continue to try to teach me unless I found my way back to loving it. I wanted to stop playing because of my mother's emotional outburst after I had tried out for the town talent show. As a child I did not want to witness another display of my mother's angst over me being upset when I had the problem at my audition. Her meltdown after the incident was too much for me to bear. I remember an incident with my son that exemplifies how a mother should respond to an issue like this. I had driven him to school to prepare for the first performance of his first musical in high school. In the car he had told me that he was very nervous about the performance. I smiled at him and lovingly explained to him that it was fine and also normal to feel nervous at a time like this in life. He smiled back at me, got out of the car, and ran to the building and never looked back.

We certainly were not well off but as a family we always had everything we needed. But our mother constantly complained about what was wrong with her life. And she was always negative believing that others were always better off than we were. Her favorite saying was "think happy thoughts" and she had many books on the subject of feeling happy but they never did any good. As she aged it seemed that she was never satisfied with the things we did for her and she was not supportive of her family. I believe this had a very negative effect on both of us as children and that she had an even worse effect on my brother as he grew into an adult. So, yes, our mother's attitude towards life was a detrimental factor to us.

Once, when Ken was away, my mother invited the children and me over for dinner. I explained that they were in final rehearsals for the high school musical and the rehearsals might run a little late so she shouldn't expect us for dinner until 6:30 p.m. When we arrived on time I could tell by her demeanor that she was upset that we hadn't arrived sooner. At dinner she talked exclusively about what was happening in her own life and showed absolutely no interest in the upcoming musical that was so important to the boys and to me. The boys were having an enjoyable time recounting to each other the funny things that had happened at the rehearsal. She became so annoyed with them that she finally blurted out, "I am talking here and you are loud and you keep interrupting me. If you don't stop it right now I will not invite you over for dinner again!"

With that my oldest son exclaimed to his brother, "Do you hear that! We won't ever have to come over here for dinner again!" They were laughing and high-fiving each other! She calmed down and finally realized that there were others in the room besides her. The next day she actually called to apologize to each of the boys for her behavior. Most of us love our grandchildren in the most beautiful and precious way. I always say I love being a grandparent and it is such a special relationship because all I have to do is love them. My mother never showed that kind of feeling to our sons.

I could not say that my parents had a happy marriage. I never saw any love between them. I very rarely saw them laugh with each other or seem to enjoy each other in any loving way. It seemed that they just existed in their marriage. I can't remember any times when they looked forward to being alone together and, although my grandmother was almost always available to babysit, they rarely went out together and never went away as a couple. We did have many wonderful family vacations. We almost always went away with our cousins to New Hampshire or to the beach in New Jersey and, as children, we had great times.

My father hated television and the movies and always thought the world was a mess and only getting worse with each passing day. They were very uptight and righteous and I never heard either of them swear. They said they were devout Christians and much of their lives and social lives revolved around the church. But I certainly never saw any Christian values surrounding them and making them feel at peace and accepting of their situation in life. This was how I grew up.

At the time I started therapy I was also finally realizing that there was much more, in addition to the obvious. I was always exhausted. I just could not handle everything in my life. I never thought the therapist relationship would work for me because I felt very strongly that I was beyond help. But I would not give up trying to find out what was wrong with me, what was imbedded deep into my soul, so I could improve my life and at least try to have the best life I could for me and my wonderful family. In retrospect I have no idea where I found the courage to even try therapy. I was so downtrodden and certainly did not feel worthy of help or even worthy enough to ask for help. I also felt abandoned for much of my adult life and impossible to help. Just imagine how defeated I was that it took me nine years of trying over and over again to understand that I finally had someone to help me.

My married life was wonderful but what I was trying to cope with at this time in my life was much more than anything that Ken could help me with. I could feel comfortable and safe for the most part during the therapy sessions, but after each session was over all of my doubts and insecurities came back. Trust is a short five-letter word; but when you lose it, in the core of your being, as such a young child and knowing that you have no one in your childhood home to protect you and help you, it becomes an immense struggle to finally accept help and because you are sure that no one would want to help a filthy, dirty, disgusting, useless, and undeserving person like me. I thought of myself as a piece of garbage. But somehow I had the courage to try. I also had the tenacity to suffer the unbelievable pain for the sake of my future. The depth and breadth of my tenacity was immeasurable. This is just part of the unbelievable horror that sexual abuse survivors suffer.

I need to say something now. Right now. For all of you who have suffered these indignities in your own life or for those of you who know someone who has, whether you know them from close contact or from afar, you need to learn from me now, at this very moment, that you have the capacity to finally understand at some level what I am talking about. And to get it. And to never forget this. To never ever forget this for as long as you live.

We, all of us, need to take these horrors out of the darkness. We need to stop the recoiling, the denying, the cover-ups, the listening but not hearing, and the dismissal of these accusations. The seriousness of our sweeping this under the rug, not taking our discoveries to the authorities, not following through to help the innocents in our society must stop. And we must stop excusing this behavior because it is too painful to be discussed, to be believed, to be recognized, to be addressed, and finally to be changed. We must begin to understand that this type of abuse affects people for their entire lives, regardless of the help they receive. Most of all, we need to be aware that all forms of abuse in people's lives stay with them FOREVER, even after it is dealt with. It is always there and can come to the surface at any time. The therapy helps us to know when it has re-appeared and how to deal with it, but does not help us to be completely free of the ramifications of the abuse. That does not happen. It is always part of us. Just as if we had a physical injury that never healed completely.

As I said, once I got into therapy it was horrible and painful and frightening to see myself under the microscope, laid out for everyone it seemed to laugh at, to criticize, and to further substantiate my feelings that I had no self-worth. Understand that these were my feelings, not the feelings of the two therapists I saw during this journey. But I thought so little of myself and I was so incredibly needy in my core in that I longed to confront the pain from my past, that even when I was with the people that I supposedly could trust, many times I trusted less instead of feeling in a safe place. These feelings of mistrust originated on the day when I was eight years old when my father said, "Nobody cares what I do to you. I don't love you, no one loves you, and no one will ever love you."

But there were always two who loved me throughout my life including my grandmother (she loved me until she died when I was 42 years old and she was 100 years old, and even today she is always with me) and my husband, who I never doubted loved me for all these years. But I still ask him at least five times a day, sometimes 20 times a day "Do you love me?" And he always answers me, "Yes, I do love you," and never has said to me, "Why do you keep asking me this?" Boy, did I choose wisely when I married him. He knows so strongly in his heart that I always need this reassurance from him to keep me knowing that I am valuable as a person, not only to him, but also to my children and grandchildren and the wider world.

Have you ever heard of the concept of the inner child? In therapy you discover that there are two parts of yourself. One is an adult who has a husband to take care of, then children and a home and a career; and the other is this child, your inner child, who has never matured and grown beyond being an innocent child. You carry your inner child around with you all of the time, with all of her immaturity and childish ways and lack of trust and PAIN, pain from her past when she did not have the proper support and love that she deserved. She has never been able to make the transition that normal people make from childhood to adulthood. She is the one who needs the therapy and the healing in order to become a complete adult. Never forget, however, that she cannot do any of this alone. You, the adult, must be there to love her, guide her, reassure her, and comfort her during this process.

In the beginning I began therapy because I was struggling again with the panic attacks that had plagued me for my adult life. My notes on the meetings say that I rarely think of myself or put myself above others or ask for help. Here I was trying to be perfect, the perfect mother, wife, daughter, sister, financial advisor, and never wanting to let others down. But this attitude and behavior took a toll on me. It never occurred to me that I should be any other way. I always tried to please everyone and now, in this new relationship, I was trying to please the therapist, too, instead of pleading for his help. I would try to say what I thought he wanted to hear. And, I was totally baffled by this new relationship in my life. Here was someone who did not want anything from me. All he wanted was to help me. It took a while for me to understand this phenomenon. At any rate, we started with the panic attacks as that was why I had come to see him. People experience panic attacks because they cannot handle their "fight or flight" response to the things that happen in their daily lives. Part of the job of the therapist is to help the patient understand the triggers that cause the panic response and to learn to fight and not to run. In other words to find real solutions to handling life.

I also was trying to accept that thoughts are not actions and thoughts are not sins. I could have bad thoughts about people but that did not make me a bad or imperfect person. I also could feel that I had some unresolved conflicts that I needed to come to grips with. Getting all of the negative energy out was a healthy thing and not something I should be ashamed of. Of course I never knew in these early stages how much negative energy I had to purge before I could be okay with myself in my own skin. And I never realized that I needed to discover and recall these issues myself and that the therapist, even though he knew what these issues were long before I did, had to wait until I was able to uncover this all on my own, with his help. Of course this mainly included the issues surrounding the sexual abuse.

He once told me that everything is revealed in the first visit and that he knew that first day that something very serious had happened to me but of course not exactly what. Survivors of sexual abuse, like me, typically go to therapy to find out what is wrong **with them** and not what was done wrong **to them**. My main issues and one of the first things that I learned about myself was that I could be so strong and courageous in helping others but I was always unable to help myself. I never failed anyone who needed help from me except myself. If someone did something wrong to me I was unable to stand up for myself in any way from the simplest to the most egregious wrongs. This was because I had no self-worth. But I was always a champion of helping others.

At this point it may be helpful for those of you who have never been in therapy to understand more deeply how the therapist relationship works, specifically in difficult relationships such as the one I had with my therapist. My relationship with the therapist was difficult because of the terrible trauma that I had suffered as a child. At the basis of any patient-therapist relationship there is the issue of transference. This means that, at some points, the therapist can be the bad people in your life. Or, at some points, the therapist can be the good people that you wish had been in your life to help you with your problems and your development during your childhood. This transference helps the patient uncover deeply-held emotions and events and these discovered feelings can be transferred to the therapist. When the therapist tries to help you, he or she helps you by transference in the relationship. This relationship provides a safe place and space for the patient to uncover powerful and usually hurtful, difficult issues. The patient then comes to a better understanding of his or her own present emotional attitudes.

For example, when I was rediscovering my relationship with my father, at times the therapist became my father during our time together. Transference also helps the patient to find peace with what has happened in childhood and to learn to navigate difficult times in the present. The patient needs to understand this and to come to peace with the transference during the therapeutic relationship. And so the relationship can feel wonderful and peaceful and safe at times and then fraught with anxiety and pain and hurt at other times. A good therapist listens to all you have to say and sticks with you no matter how hurt you are, how much you cry and cry out, no matter how awful some of the things you say to the therapist are. They stick by you and keep reassuring you that you are in a safe place and that you will not be harmed no matter how bad things are and how painful the sessions are. And I was truly in a safe place, even though at times it did not feel that way.

Here is a simple example of that. Once when I arrived in the waiting room at the therapist's office, the radio was playing classical music (remember that my father played violin). All of a sudden I began to have intense feelings of fright and unease. I did not know what to do. As I sat there I felt worse and worse about the music playing in the waiting room until it became so unbearable, I had to escape. It was all I could do to sit there and wait for the therapist to open his office door and call me in for the session. All of a sudden he came out. He could see I was very upset. As I sat down he asked me what was wrong. I told him about the radio. He asked me what I could have done to change the situation in the waiting room to make myself more comfortable. I told him I could have left and run away. He gently told me I could have changed the radio station. I looked at him like he had just solved the world nuclear crisis.

This illustrates how serious these minor situations can become in therapy and in life when you are so insecure. It also is the key to understanding panic attacks. There is a trigger that causes them. To be able to stop them you need to know how to turn off the trigger. In this case it was as simple as turning off the radio. I spent a great deal of time in therapy with the help of the therapist learning how to turn off these triggers. The assurances I received many, many times by the therapist were real and realistic, and I can say unequivocally that I was always safe, although I did not always feel safe. And today, I truly love the violin and can enjoy hearing it played in any situation.

In the early days of therapy, I wrote about my anxiety. I questioned myself by saying, "Why can't I just relax and enjoy life? Who am I trying to impress? What is eating away at me?" I had a lot to learn, didn't I? I also wrote about the therapist telling me that I had to handle this anxiety myself, my response being I didn't want to handle it, I want him to handle it for me. And him telling me, "Do something for yourself." He was telling me that I needed to learn how to deal with my "fight or flight" response to anxiety. I needed to find ways inside of myself. And I needed to fight and not to run. That would be the answer to my panic attacks. I needed to learn how to change my responses to the panic situations with real solutions so I could handle life much easier. One example I recall is when I would be in a store and Ken and I would go to different departments to pick up items that we needed. If I couldn't find him immediately after I found what I needed, I would begin to panic and many times when I finally found him, we had to leave the store because I was so insecure and panic stricken. With the help I received I was able to overcome these panic feelings and just breathe until I found him. Now it is not a problem.

I kept asking him and thinking why can't *we* deal with this, why can't *we* figure out how to get over it, past it, and around it? Obviously I didn't know that I had to discover what had happened to me and then he would help me deal with it. It was buried so deeply in my psyche. But discovery came first. He was there patiently waiting for me to come to grips with my childhood and the discoveries I needed to make in order to work through them and to finally heal. It was to be a long and difficult road with many twists and turns.

To say that he had patience with me would be an understatement. As I wound myself down this long, twisted, and tortuous road he stood by me. Besides our weekly sessions I would be call him and write letters to him to share a range of emotions. And he was always there for me. My neediness must have been such a professional burden to him as it was always there and always so strong. This went on for several years. Can you imagine being hounded by a patient in such an intense way for such a long time? When I was there with him I felt safe, but when I left I was almost immediately back to the anxiety and insecurity that I longed to escape.

Along the way I had many theories about my childhood and what had happened. One was about a dentist whom my mother took me to see. I had terrible teeth so I visited the dentist often. There was something creepy about this dentist and some things that were inappropriate about his behavior, especially the way he touched my face. I asked my mother to please take me to another dentist but she refused. Another disappointment in my life with my mother.

Many other incidents from my childhood surfaced over many months but then I remembered something that one of my college professors said to me. Wilson College was a small liberal arts school and I majored in economics. The department was so small that we only had two economics professors. Those of us majoring in economics (there were six economics majors in my class) got to know our professors both very well. They were mentors and friends. One day I was in the professor's office and he looked at me and said, "You know, you have talked about everyone in your life but you have never said one word about your father." I remembered this comment in therapy and it triggered the memories of what my father had done to me and how my mother had never been supportive of me.

I will never forget the day I was finally able to put into words what had exactly happened to me the first time I was sexually abused by my father. I was lying on the therapist's couch in the fetal position and quietly told him what had happened to me. I didn't want to tell him, but he softly spoke to me and made me understand that just this once I needed to say it out loud. It was truly awful, almost as awful as when it happened to me. Afterwards, after leaving his office the sting of my own guilt and shame felt like they would combine and set me on fire. I hated the fact that I had shared this pain with another person and I was horrified that he knew. It was awful and almost too much to bear. But, in spite of everything, I was finally free. I had taken the first step to real freedom. I knew how much my inner child had suffered and I knew that I was finally at the beginning of healing her.

Unfortunately "at the beginning of healing her" lasted for several more years. The angst, the depression, the uncertainty of how my life would evolve after this revelation all lay ahead of me and my family. And to this day things come up that bring me back to that dark place. Because all of this was still a work in progress (and always will be) and I had many more experiences ahead of me until I had finished this work to mean that it really made a difference in my life.

There was a time when I brought my husband to therapy with me so I could tell him in a safe place what sex had meant to me as that helpless child. While I was telling him he sat there crying his heart out. I did not stop to comfort him. I had to get it all out, just this once, and he knew that I needed to tell him what the horrors of the sexual abuse had done to me. As I sat there watching him wrestle with what I was saying I told him everything. I remember him saying, with his teeth clenched, and his hands shaped in fists, "I want to kill your father" over and over again.

During the course of our long marriage we have loved each other deeply and passionately. There have been times when a sexual relationship has been difficult for me but we have learned that there are many ways to love and care for each other. When things have been rough for me he has always been immensely and deeply understanding and has never forced me to do anything that was upsetting to me. Do not stay in a relationship where this is not the case. You are vulnerable and should never be forced to feel you are anyone's sexual slave.

I remember some time after this visit to the therapist with Ken that I decided to tell the children so they would have a better understanding of their mother and what made her tick. For example, why I spent some weekends in bed not being able to face the days. Why I needed to be insulated from real life at times and to just be in a state of almost suspended animation so I could be free of the thoughts and feelings that interrupted and disrupted my life almost all of the time. The memories, the flashbacks, the times when I reverted back to my childhood feelings of unworthiness and despair plagued me. So, one Saturday afternoon I told them. It was the first time I had told anyone except for my husband and my therapist. I remember they were around twelve and fourteen and they were innocent children.

They had been well treated and taken care of during their childhoods. They knew very little of real life and certainly none of real life without the protection of the most caring and compassionate and protective parents any two children could have. We loved them and cared for them and accepted them as they were. We helped them and held them throughout their times of trial, always there for them in every way possible. Was life always good, no! But they each, in their own way, knew that we were there for them and that we accepted them with all of their strengths and weaknesses. So, it was time for me to share something about my life that was truly foreign to them. What I said is not important but I believe their reactions, which were so different, speak volumes about them.

One of my sons got up and quietly walked around the house and gathered all photos of his grandfather and put them in a drawer, and the other son respectfully asked questions such as, "How could this happen? Why didn't anyone help you? What did you do?" It was not as difficult as I thought. They were both so respectful and understanding and I believe that they "got it" right away. I love my boys so much. They were like little soul mates of mine, like best friends of mine, two people I could really talk to and who could understand me and get it. After that day we never spoke about it again in any kind of graphic way and they never asked me any probing questions. Yet I knew that they would be able to understand me and especially why I could and would retreat from life and those around me when I needed to and had to do so.

As I said earlier the therapy lasted for many years. During the course of my therapy my therapist told me about a female therapist in our area who had been sexually abused herself and told me that she had group therapy for a group of women who had also been sexually abused. He thought it would be good for me to join this group and see if it would help me with all of the issues that I faced. I was very scared by this idea and horrified by the thought of ever sharing what had happened to me with others. I screamed at my therapist and told him that I would never think of going to this group therapy that he spoke to me about. However, in the end, after a great deal of thought and persuasion by the therapist, I decided to try it. I joined the group and it was a positive step in my recovery. Of course, it was also difficult for me but I had enough self-awareness and understanding at this time that I could opt out of activities that upset me; that was a giant step for me. For example, I remember that one time she asked us all to draw something and I just felt I couldn't do it and I told her so. She said it was all right and that I could stay on the sidelines during this activity. Do you know how much strength it took for me to ask to be excused from the activity? For me it was a real moment of seeing how far I had come; rather than feeling uncomfortable about doing something, I could say no.

During the time I was in regular therapy and group therapy, I wrote about how I was doing so much better in my life during the day. I even learned a trick to control the panic attacks. I found out that if I told Ken that I was feeling like I was going to have a panic attack, I immediately felt better just by the act of sharing my feelings. That certainly was progress for me. However, I was constantly shaken during the night when I was asleep. I was having terrible dreams. It was as if my wonderful present that I worked so hard to find was being destroyed in my dreams every night. I was working so hard to put my past in the past only to have it wiped out by these awful nightmares about things happening to my present to ruin my happy and fulfilled life. It was as though my subconscious was saying that my contentment was just an illusion about to be shattered. These types of dreams still happen to me periodically today and I have to think that they always will. It's another piece that probably still haunts many other victims of sexual abuse.

I really liked the female therapist and so I also started to see her once in a while by myself. She had a very different way of dealing with the abuse and was able to help my inner child grow into adulthood. She was very helpful to me and I was finally able to merge my two selves into an adult. I never felt the deeply emotional connection to her that I had felt with my male therapist because of all of the painful and difficult discoveries I had made with him. We spoke of my issues in a very practical and non-emotional way with an emphasis on how to relieve my life stresses with practical methods that would help me cope with everyday life. Understand that I greatly missed the emotional connection that I had with the other therapist. But that part of my therapy was for the most part over and I needed to find a way to break the emotionally fraught ties that I had with my longtime male therapist.

After some time when I was still seeing my original male therapist, I believe he had become entrenched as my abusive father. We seemed to be at odds with one another and nothing seemed to help. In a very traumatic way I finally left him because I needed to get away from him. Of course it was an awful way to end my many years with him. He had always told me that our relationship would end in a good way. I believed him when he told me that I could trust that he would be there for me and that he would never let the relationship have a terrible and traumatic ending. But that is how it ended for me. In my mind he was no longer the "therapist" who had been kind and caring and soft and healing but had entrenched himself in my thoughts as "the rapist" and I told him so. I wished for a very long time that it could have been different after all of the years we were together but it was not to be so. This break caused me a great deal of anxiety and grief; but somehow, especially with the love and care of my husband and children, I was able to muddle through it. But at least he found me a new therapist before I had to leave him and I was very grateful for this. This had made it possible for me to leave him. I believe that he knew that I needed to move on from him. And so I finished my therapy with the female therapist and finally felt it was time to go it alone and end therapy.

I do not wish this wrenching end to therapy for anyone out there. However, this taught me once again that I am not alone and that I am strong and that wherever you are in life you can find someone to help you. Most of all you can count on yourself. That is one of the great lessons that I hope you can take away from this book. You are never alone in life. If we study the most successful people in the world we find that most of them have faced overwhelming obstacles in their lives that have shaped their thinking and have been at the core of their success. I came to a deeper understanding of why I always loved reading about the lives of real people. If you doubt me, read some biographies and autobiographies of great people that you admire and you will find this truth is reality. If they can make it so can you!

thirteen

My Own Office

*I*n January of 1990 I struck out on my own and opened an office in our hometown of Fair Haven, New Jersey. It was wonderful for me to finally be able to have my own space and to be able to do things in my own way. I was so happy to move forward in my life. It was a huge step both personally and professionally. Ken and I made quite a financial commitment to the business with the costs of the initial rental and deposit and the purchase of furniture and equipment for the office. My wonderful grandmother was still alive when I made the decision to open my own office. I remember very well how my conversation about this big step went with my grandmother and my mother. At the time my grandmother was in a nursing home as her care was too much for my mother to handle on her own. I began to tell them both about my new endeavor together because I had learned not to talk about these serious subjects with my mother alone because her reactions were always so negative. As I told them what I was about to embark on my mother immediately began to push back saying, "Oh no, this is not a good time to do this; the economy is not doing well and you should not put all of this money into your own business now."

My grandmother's reaction was immediate and firm. "Oh Edythe, will you please shut up! She knows what she's doing and I have no doubts that she will be successful." It was so great to have someone from my own family on my side, besides Ken, who was behind this move wholeheartedly. After my grandmother died, I learned to always call my mother-in-law first about anything that could be controversial so I would get solid support from someone before speaking to my mother.

I have always said that people who start their own businesses would have been the first ones on the wagon train if they had been around when the West was being settled. You have to have a certain crazy spirit to take this step. I knew that many businesses that have been started have failed and that this was a possibility. But I also felt that I could succeed if I worked hard and stayed true to myself in the way I felt about my profession and where it was headed, and, how I carried out my professional duties with my clients. I could finally treat people in the way they deserved to be treated by those in the financial planning and the tax preparation profession. It was absolutely liberating to be able to handle situations in my own way and break away from my former partner and the baggage that she had foisted on me for so many years. Of course I also had the entire responsibility of my actions and decisions in the business solely on my shoulders. But I loved it.

In the beginning, I was struggling with all of the issues in my life while I was trying to start a business. I remember many days when all I did was sit there and wait for the telephone to ring, when I was unable to do anything proactive to get the business up and running. But that was okay. It was so heavenly to be away from my former partner and the way she behaved and spoke to and about her clients. I remember one particular incident that really brings this into focus. She had purchased carpeting from a local store with which she had a very close relationship. When the installer was an hour late in arriving at her residence, she called the store and screamed at them about the lateness of their installer and then began to berate the installer whom she knew personally, telling the store manager that the installer was a drunk and she would not allow him to proceed with the installation if she smelled any alcohol on his breath. It was awful. The installer arrived shortly after this call. He breezed in, happy and ready to begin the installation of the carpet. He was totally taken aback by her nasty tone. He was fine, perfectly sober, and explained that the prior job had taken more time than originally anticipated. He proceeded to begin the job and happily completed it in no time. I forced my ex-partner to call the store and apologize about her earlier conversation. I carefully explained that this could cost him his job. She did so but this is just one example of what I lived with every day while I worked with her.

I remember that of course she was very angry with me that I had left her. At one point, in an effort to smooth things over between us, the broker that we used for our investment business invited us to meet in his office to see if he could resolve this breach between us. I agreed to go to the meeting. As soon as it started she began to say all kinds of ridiculous things about our relationship. I became so angry that I stood up, leaned over and banged my open hand on the conference table and told her I was finished listening to all of her crazy talk.

Afterward I remembered how my father had done the same thing to me, banging his fist on his desk, so many years before. I was finally free of that memory.

The long and short of the meeting was that she had cheated me out of money that she owed me and I would not sit and listen to her inane comments about our relationship. With that I gathered up my papers and left the room. I was finished once and for all with her crazy behavior.

Sometime after that the broker, who held weekly meetings in the office, said that I would be able to attend these meetings every other week and she would be able to attend the other meetings when I was not there. This really did not set well with me. I was very upset about this. I had no problem sitting across the table from her at meetings and I did not feel that it was right that I had to miss out on these important meetings because of her. The broker agreed with me when I expressed these feelings to him and I was able to attend any and all meetings that I cared to attend. This greatly angered her and she soon moved to another broker. I always felt that this was a big victory for me in that the broker had decided to do the right thing even though, at the time, he would be losing the bigger producer (my partner) while doing the right thing morally and using good business practices. I mentioned this to every member of our group at the retirement party for this broker, and I will never forget what a good man he was.

Having my own office and my own space was such a wonderful feeling. It was not at all difficult for me to believe what was happening to me at the time. Of course, before the break, I had consulted with an attorney to find out the proper way to make the break in terms of the clients. My attorney told me that clients that I had dealt with exclusively as either tax or financial planning clients had a right to know that I had left the previous firm and where I was now. I was able to send them a letter to that effect just giving the minimum of information including the date that I changed my office and the name and address of the new entity. I did not ask them to stay with me but just informed them of my new circumstances. It would be up to them to move to the new location with me or stay and do their business at the old location with her.

Almost everyone chose to continue with me and those who did not want to drive the 15 miles to the new location would be serviced by me with home visits that would not be a problem for me. So, I was up and running. And since I had started in January and it was the beginning of tax season, I was soon busy with appointments which were a help to me in getting started. I also advertised the new location to encourage people in the new area to come to see me.

I don't honestly recall any numbers for my first season there, but I do know that it was successful right from the start. I did not need to infuse the business with any more of our personal funds after our initial outlay and was soon showing a profit, which steadily increased over the years. I started teaching financial planning courses in the evenings for the local communities at the local high schools and the local community college and also at Rutgers University in New Brunswick, New Jersey. I also belonged to many tax and financial planning organizations and participated in classes and lectures at libraries and other civic centers. I really enjoyed teaching so much and loved meeting new people. I added many new clients through these avenues and a great majority of them stayed on for many years. My practice grew and grew until I had three people working with me, and I had expanded in my original location by adding three additional rooms to my suite of offices.

I was genuinely so happy with my business. And I was feeling strong and confident. I had completed my therapy by now and the issues that had affected me before were moving from the forefront to the background. The therapy and the grappling with all of the issues in my life were falling into place and I was finally feeling much better. Were there still issues in my life? Yes, in all places and times things would come up for me and still do, but I was mostly able to realize what was happening and I was able to handle the situations. Sometimes, because of the place I was in at the time, I lost clients but that was fine and I learned to forgive myself for these times. Usually it was because I was not responding to them quickly enough. I tried to let this go when it happened. It was difficult but I had learned so much about myself and also learned that I needed to forgive myself. This is an important lesson that those of us who had these difficult things happen to us must never forget. Our lives and, in this case, our careers will never go in a straight line; and we must always be ready to forgive ourselves and move on. This is also a time when those around us can be a great help and comfort to us.

I truly loved my clients, each in their own way, and was so happy to help them through all of the financial decisions that they had to make. I planned many retirements, college saving plans, new car purchases, home remodeling projects, business startups and expansions, divorces (which became a real specialty for me in later years), deaths of spouses and other relatives, moving and relocating homes and or businesses, and any other financial issues that my clients had to deal with in their lives. Also, having knowledge of the tax implications of all of these issues was very helpful to the clients and saved them money as well. For me it was a perfect fit and my clients became friends over the many years together.

Many times I was helping three generations by the end of my years in practice. I used to have the young clients come in for a money discussion before they attended college, which I truly enjoyed. I also told the students if they had any questions they could call me and I would help and I would not tell their parents. Actually, this was one of my serious pledges to clients when I opened the business and that was that I would never even tell anyone that they were clients of mine and if some of them knew each other they never heard that I was servicing their friend or relative from me. Some of my mother's friends became clients and she could never understand why she didn't know that until they (the clients) told her themselves. I knew so much about so many clients. I never even told Ken. I knew that if I told no one, I didn't have to worry about what I had said or not said.

In addition, I knew everything about them. I am the kind of person that people feel they can tell me anything and everything, many times on the first meeting, and it is still like that with me. I go to a new hairdresser, for example, and before I go home I have heard an entire life story. I wonder, *"Why does everyone tell me everything about themselves on our first meeting?"* It still happens all of the time. I think it happens because of my past which certainly shaped the way I approach people and how I present myself to people who feel I can be trusted to care and help them. In my business it was a true blessing for me and my clients that I could get so close to them, so quickly.

What anyone says and how it is said is a true window into their soul. Whether you agree with them or disagree with them is not as important as understanding what drives their opinions and their choices in life. Rather than judging people, I always tried to understand where they were coming from. It was an important part of my profession to make them feel comfortable with me and to develop a deeper understanding of what was important to them. I always felt that I learned how to be like this from being on the high school debating team. When we went to meets we never knew which side of the issue we would be on, so we had to understand and to be able to support each side with precision and fervor.

I had pledged to myself and to my clients that I would always do what was best for them and not what would earn me the most money. I also took on any client, no matter how rich or poor. I pledged to myself that I would help anyone. I was brutally honest with them about all of their issues. I was there to help them do the correct thing for them and their families. I settled many arguments between spouses, among siblings about the financial care of their parents and financial issues after the parent's death, and I taught people in debt what was important in life. I would often tell clients who had spending issues that once we have food, clothing, and shelter we have everything that we need and all of the rest is just extras that we really don't need. I helped people who had debts of more than $100,000 get out of debt. I often cut up people's credit cards right in front of them with their mouths open.

As an aside, it was also wonderful that I was in the same town where our children went to school. They always knew where I was and that they could come and see me after school if they needed me. I could also help them by bringing things they had forgotten to school. Here is a funny story that we still laugh about today. Sometimes I would have computer issues and would call my son out of his class to the school office to ask him questions. Once I even went to school and stood at his classroom window waving at him to come out and help me with a computer problem. I remember once a teacher asked him upon his return to class, "Was that really necessary?" and my son would always answer, "Yes."

After I was in Fair Haven for many years, the World Trade Center twin towers in New York were destroyed and everything changed in the business. It was a nightmare for everyone in the country but for our area, with so many people who worked in New York City, it was really a tragedy that hit close to home. We lost so many lives in our area and the financial markets were a mess and so my business was at a new critical place. I held many hands and cried many tears. As a matter of fact, Ken lost his job in New York City as the company moved its operations to Providence, Rhode Island. So we were faced with another life decision. We could have moved to Rhode Island, but we did not want to move since my business was doing so well. So, being a little unnerved about what to do next, we talked to some business associates who had been working together as husband and wife, and they assured us that it would also be a good move for us. Shortly after that Ken came to work with me in 2002.

Soon after, another big change happened. I was sitting at my desk one afternoon when the representative for the company that now owned the building where we were renting came in to see me. He asked me why I had not responded to the registered letter he had sent to me. I had not responded to his letter because I had never received it. He informed me that the company needed the entire property for their business and that all renters had to leave the property by November 1 of that year. I could not believe it after having been there so many years and being so happy and comfortable there. However, change is one of the things that we can all be assured of during our lives, so we would have to deal with it. By this time the children had both graduated from college so being close to home was not an issue.

So we started looking for places to rent. After going to many properties we finally found an office condominium complex that was in our area (about twelve miles from our house) that suited our needs, and we rented the property from the condominium owner. After we were there for a year we decided to buy the property as we were very happy there in that location. The clients that we had moved closer to were happy, and the ones who were now farther away were not so happy, but I was willing to visit them at their homes if the drive was an issue. In addition the property was closer to the major highways in the area and so many of the clients were very happy about that. It was easier for many of them to get to us since our office would be on their way home from work as well. I believe the connection to the highways also brought in more referrals to the business.

I had so many experiences with clients. First and foremost I tried to make them feel welcome and treasured. I had clients from all faiths and backgrounds, from all racial backgrounds, gay and straight clients and transgender clients, rich and poor clients. Anyone who needed help was welcome to come through my doors. I went to court with clients and fought for their rights with everything I had accompanying them to financial regulations court in New York City when they had been wronged by a previous advisor. I took them to probate when a loved one died, met with their attorneys and changed the course of their wills and trusts on many occasions since I had financial as well as tax knowledge to help with these issues. When people were poor but had issues that needed to be addressed, I often helped them pro bono or for a minimum charge. I never turned people away. If clients had lost their jobs and were currently unemployed I would file their tax returns for free. However, I was not really running a charity! For every kind thing that I did for clients I was re-paid in kind. For example, I once helped someone with a difficult tax issue for next to nothing and two weeks later she referred someone to me who had a large rollover to be invested. It always happened that way.

I had several people who came to me over the years who had not filed their tax returns for multiple years, as many as ten years without filing. This was a difficult task but I was up to it even though it took many hours to complete. It also usually required many telephone calls with the I.R.S., and I remember that they always were surprised that I had all of the original forms going back to the prior years. Many times having the old forms was a help because some of the tax laws had changed, but I was able to use the old laws since I had the forms. Can you imagine how difficult it was for someone to come in and tell me they had not filed returns for so many years? I never concentrated on why they hadn't filed but just assured them that I was there to help them and to straighten out their income tax issues. I also made my clients understand that no matter the issues with the Internal Revenue Service that might come up due to the late filings that I was there to help them all the way.

I also participated in many audits where I visited the I.R.S. offices and sometimes the auditors came to my office. My self-confidence in these areas was so helpful to the clients. I often took the audits to appeal if I wasn't satisfied with the results or the attitudes of the auditors. Remember that I was not able to fight for myself but I could fight ferociously for others. I did this with the I.R.S. by being extremely well organized and knowing all of the laws regarding the issues that would come up. I enjoyed that work immensely and had many interesting stories about working with the Internal Revenue Service. There are several interesting stories about audits that stand out in my mind.

Once I was in my office and an auditor who lived in the area dropped by. I had already received the paperwork that there was going to be an audit on the return in question that I had not prepared. When the auditor came into my office I said to her, "Well, there is one thing that we can get straight right away, and that is that this return under audit is a completely bogus return and we both know it." I think that surprised her to say the least. I reconstructed the return properly and the client did owe money but he knew that would be the case. As a matter of fact, we even turned in the former preparer to the IRS criminal investigation unit.

Another time a client came to me who was being audited because she had claimed her grandchildren as dependents, and she was a therapist who had her own business and was being audited based on that as well. She said periodically she had patients who were audited and she said she wanted to go with me to the audit so she could explain to her patients what it was like. I organized her entire return and carefully explained to her that she could not ask any questions of the auditor and that she could not answer any questions asked by the auditor. I would re-phrase the auditor's questions in the way I wanted them answered. I told her if she started talking or answering, I would gently kick her in the leg to remind her to stop talking. It was not easy for her to be quiet so I did have to revert to letting her know it was time for her to be quiet! Also I always presented the client's expenses in the order of the categories that had the best receipts to show that the deductions taken on the return were correct. No changes were made to this return. After the audit was completed the auditor smiled and told us that it was the first audit that he had ever done. Nothing had been changed on this return.

Another time I had an audit that was done by an auditor who did not like me. So, every time the auditor said that he didn't agree with the amount listed on the return I just said, "Okay, we will just take this issue to the Appeals Officer." This was an extremely complicated return because the client had eight rental properties at the time. When we met with the Appeals Officer it was in the local IRS office since the appeals officer lived in that area. The Appeals Officer decided to have the original auditor in on the appeal. Every time the auditor brought up a deduction that he wanted to exclude, I was able to show why it was still a legitimate deduction. After about two hours of this, the Appeals Officer told us to go back to the waiting room and wait for him. So we packed up our boxes of records and carried them downstairs to the IRS waiting room. In the meantime the Appeals Officer had taken the auditor into the manager's office with the manager present and proceeded to scream at the auditor for 45 minutes while we waited in the waiting room. We could not hear the words that were spoken, but we knew that the auditor was not having a good day for sure! After that was over the Appeals Officer came out and told us that he was sorry but we would have to finish another day. What a scene that was!

And, lastly, we had a client who called us and told us about her brother who was being audited and she was trying desperately to get him to come to us. He was not having much luck with his tax preparer during the audit process, and she was sure that we could do better. The brother finally called us and we agreed to drive one hour up to their location. The husband and wife owned and managed a jewelry store, and the audit was going to be quite complicated because of the nature of the business and because the bookkeeping was not up to normal standards. They basically had their own way of doing it so it was a chore to make it comply with IRS standards. After meeting with them I did take on the case. It was a very successful business but again, complex to undo the bookkeeping and present the numbers in a way that reflected the proper standards. At the time they were being audited for two years. The auditor agreed to come to my office for the audit. We had individual papers all over the place and also many stacks of receipts and forms. There were too many to just keep them all in my office, and it was a chore to organize and present everything to the auditor. The clients had come over early and we were ready when the auditor knocked at the office door. As I was letting her in and exchanging pleasantries, she asked me why the clients had changed accountants. I said, "Why, does that matter?" She answered "no" so we proceeded to my office and my piles and piles of paper. We finished the first year which took about three and a half hours. After explaining to the clients who were present but not in my office during the audit how it had all worked out, the auditor stated that she had to get going back to her office. The client began to cry because he wanted to have it all completed that day. It was sad and I felt terrible. So I asked the auditor when she absolutely had to leave, and after she answered me and I asked her if we couldn't finish on that day as everything else was organized as it had been for the year we had just completed, and she looked at me and then at the client and she agreed to do it. We finished the second year and it was over and the client knew what he would owe so he could rest comfortably after that. As I took the auditor back to the front door of the office she turned to me and said, "Now I know why the clients changed accountants."

Another thing that I learned was how to write letters. Most of the audits or queries from the government agencies were answered in writing, and my answers had to be concise and very clear and to the point. It was really an art to write these letters. I remember I received a call from one of the state auditors who told me that my letter was all she needed to complete the case and she thanked me for making her job so easy. Of course that was the idea, that the auditors had everything laid out for them in a way that was correct and easy to understand.

The only reason I tell you these stories is to show how I was different I from many tax preparers because of the vulnerabilities I had in my own life. I took these issues to heart and saw to it that the clients had the proper support that they needed in every way. I was able to help people at a time in their lives when they felt they were the most vulnerable. I took my work very seriously and always tried to be at my best for the clients. In fact, if I was doing something for them that required research, I always copied the research and put it in their files so I could back up my thoughts with no problems or issues. Usually the inquiries from the Internal Revenue Service were one or two years or more after the original paperwork had been submitted so that extra bit of effort really saved time if the issues were questioned.

As a financial planner I strived to always do what was right for the client. I have had many clients over the years thank me for my efforts. Recently I had a client tell me that he owned his present house and that his daughter graduated from college with no loans because of me. I helped many people make the right decisions for them such as buying a smaller home so that it would be more affordable for them or how to chart a path to save more for their retirement. When people came in with debt many times I unceremoniously cut up their credit cards if they told me they had a difficult time not using them. I explained to clients, for example, that instead of buying an expensive gift for their parents or their wife they could paint a room or plant a garden. I told couples who needed a date night away from their children to find a couple they could switch with so they could take a picnic to the beach to spend quality time together. I explained to them that if their child wanted something they should explain to them that they would buy the item when they had the money. Many times I passed along just these practical advice tips so the people could save for long-term goals, and they were so delighted when we were able to celebrate reaching these plateaus. I remember telling a client who had lost his job to explain to his children that because he was out of work he could no longer pay them their allowance. The allowance was only a small amount, but it let the children know that they were help-ing out during a difficult time for their family. I also told clients in these situations to tell the children the family would be okay and they would not have to worry. I helped people find the best ways to finance a new kitchen or a new car. I wanted to know about each major purchase if they needed help to figure out how to pay for it or to finance it. I guess I just loved seeing people happy and helping them making the most out of their money.

I am also happy to report that never once did I receive a complaint by any of my clients that was lodged with the Securities and Exchange Commission about my work with my financial planning clients.

I truly enjoyed what I did in both the tax preparation and financial planning fields.

One day, as I was sitting in front of a long-time client and I could not remember her name, I realized that it was time to retire. I was 64 years old, but the business had taken its toll on me and it was finally time to truly enjoy life. The tax business was especially difficult with the very long hours that were involved and the fact that I had prepared taxes for all of my 35 years in the business. I believe this desire to retire was truly a message from God. After I told Ken he questioned me as to how we were going to sell the business. I said I wasn't worried about that at all, that God had it all under control. I was able to sell both businesses to people whom I knew in the tax and financial fields and to sell the office as well. Both of these advisors had come to me. I never called them or mentioned to anyone that I wanted to sell. This was, I firmly believe, a true gift from God who has helped me so many times in my life. They were also advisors who I felt would do the best for the clients. I had no issues with financial aspects of the sale as well. It was uncanny how it all worked out. And so, we retired at the end of 2013.

fourteen

The Joys of Retirement

For Ken and me, retirement has truly been a gift. I can do what I want, when I want and truly enjoy the remainder of my life. It is not always easy for me because my past still interferes with the present at times. For example, I sometimes have terribly frightening dreams that seem to be mostly about me not having control over my life. They are crazy and wild and have no basis in reality. My doctor tells me that it is the return of PSTD (Post Traumatic Stress Syndrome), and I am hopeful that this knowledge will help me overcome the dreams. For the most part this happens with less and less frequency. And I have the right people in my life to help me cope with any issues that come up, including a very strong and helpful trauma therapist. Being retired and healthy is certainly much better than working. And I know that I retired at the right time for me while I was still doing well and my practice was well valued.

We moved to Virginia to be close to our grandchildren, and that is a gift in of itself. We enjoy our time with them so much. I always say that the most wonderful thing about grandchildren is that all you have to do is love them. You are not responsible for all the mundane chores such as helping with homework, taking them to all of their activities, and all of the household chores that take up so much of Mom and Dad's time. We are also able to be there to see all of their activities such as their sports activities and school programs as they grow.

We have also enjoyed getting to know our new neighbors and becoming active members of our new community. As I write this I am the Chairwoman of the Budget and Finance Committee, a member of a committee studying the possibility of starting a non-profit entity in our community, and a member of the marketing committee to help market our community as more and more senior communities are being built around us. My husband is on the Buildings Facilities Committee for our building and on the Building and Grounds Committee for our entire complex. He also plays in the community Instrumental Ensemble. We enjoy as many of the social activities such as concerts and lectures and learning opportunities that we can. We also participate in fitness activities such as water aerobics to keep us healthy and able to enjoy life to the fullest.

We are enthusiastic travelers and try to take at least three long trips a year along with shorter adventures when the opportunity comes along. Ken has driven a few times over 2500 miles on these journeys. We have been to most of the National Parks in the country and have taken trips to Europe, Alaska, Hawaii, Iceland, the Caribbean, and Canada so far. And so, our life is happy.

In addition, we are going to church again on a regular basis after thirty-five years of severe panic attacks each and every time I have entered a church. These terrible panic attacks came from the failure of my minister when I was a child to help me when I told him about my sexual abuse at the hand of my father. I was able to go to church after but never truly felt comfortable there. But I was truly unable to attend church after the minister of the church we had been attending when the children were young was convicted of child sexual abuse and sent to prison.

When we moved to Virginia I went to a Memorial Day service where my husband was performing in the Instrumental Ensemble here. I was very impressed by the minister who spoke at this service. I later learned that he was part of the church family that was right here in the complex where we lived. I decided to try going to church there and, for some reason, I felt very comfortable there. This has truly been a gift that I am able to attend church again after so many years. I believe this is because the minister just made me feel comfortable again in the institution of church. I have always been a Christian and have tried to live my life adhering to Christian principles. It feels wonderful to be able to enjoy the church service again. As luck would have it, the minister has just been transferred to another church and we will have another minister in a few short weeks so I am faced with another challenge in my life.

I am also participating in a wonderful Bible Study group that emphasizes learning and working to make the world a better place by being a disciple of Jesus. I wonder where this will lead me.

As I conclude my book in an effort to help others overcome their incredibly difficult past horrors and trauma to have a fulfilling life, I can only hope that my words and thoughts have helped you to overcome the obstacles you have faced and have hindered you from becoming the best "you" that you can be. I also hope that any abuse victims will realize, from the experiences I have shared, that they need not feel alone and isolated. Life is certainly a journey, and we each travel on our own individual path. It has often been said that every one of us, no matter what happens on our journey, needs only one person to believe in us and to help us on this journey. I sincerely hope you will find that one person who believes in you and who can provide you with a peaceful place along your journey. If you are just starting this journey, may you understand that it will seem impossible at times and that you will be powerfully challenged along your path. But, please, don't ever give up or give in during your struggle. Take good care of yourself and never let the evil in your life take you away from all of us.

I also sincerely hope that this journey of truth that I have taken you on has helped you in some way. My greatest hope for you is that you do not let your abuser win. No matter who they are or how powerful they are, do not let your abuser take away your confidence and your ability to achieve what you want for yourself.

Finally, I also hope that those of you who are the friends, spouses, children, relatives, doctors, social workers, psychologists, psychiatrists, ministers, and other colleagues and supporters of someone who has experienced these life trials have had your eyes opened and made your understanding of abuse clearer through the words I have written here.

Epilogue

I began to suffer from Post-Traumatic Stress Disorder shortly after I finished this book. People did advise me not to write about the PTSD because the book was finished, and they also felt that it would discourage survivors to know that I could suffer again after so many years, but I feel that it is another chapter to add to my story that will show that, no matter what life sends your way, you can rise above it.

There was a word that came into my mind after I finished. I can't remember what is was but it upset me so much that I became suicidal again. Also, remembering that I had promised my husband that I would never attempt suicide, I started to think about murdering him and then killing myself.

Fortunately for me, I had a wonderful psychiatrist in my corner who I was able to tell about these thoughts. Of course he was very concerned about me. After a few weeks of appointments with him and of these and other very chilling ideas and ideations, he recommended that I enter a Partial Hospitalization Program near where I live. I was able to do this as an outpatient because my husband would be able to drive me there and pick me up after each day session. My doctor felt it wasn't safe to let me drive myself. I was there for six days. I participated with other people who were in the program during the daily seminars and sessions. Also, some of the sessions were one-on-one. I also met with the psychiatrists in the program. It was a great program and it helped me to become safe enough to finish and go home to my own psychiatrist and then on to a trauma therapist that they helped me to find at the PHP program. The trauma therapist was a wonderful addition to my group of people I can count on to be there to help me.

I learned so much about myself and my struggle over the sexual abuse as a child. I found out many things from the trauma therapist, and I think the most helpful was about ANTS, automatic negative thoughts, that people who suffer from PTSD need to understand. These are the thoughts that each of us have that pull us back to the places where we DO NOT want to be. It helped me to fill in many open and empty parts of myself. For example, I discovered that I was still thinking of my boys as children, as if I still had the right to tell them what to do or how to handle problems in their lives. For some reason, to me, they were still young and not both grown men and, of course, this had caused some interesting times between us. It seems so weird now. They were so understanding when I told them about my thoughts on this subject.

I also realized that I was too frightened to complete the phases that I needed to finish before I was ready to publish the book. I had to ask my editor to help me with some of the tasks. She was happy to help and this made that work easier for me to complete. So always remember to seek out help. There are people who are out in the world to help us.

Appendix

SOULFULLY

Reverently listening...

    To my soul opening up to you

Painfully hearing...

    My soul despairing

Wistfully wondering...

    How did my soul survive?

Acutely aware...

    Of my soul self-destructing

Intellectually trying to understand...

    The great devastation of my soul

Hopefully wishing...

    You could protect my soul – then and now

In frustration pondering...

    What can you do now to ease my soul's suffering?

Please don't doubt what you have done for me…

    I have come to you and said, "Please hold
    my soul in your hands,"

And you have answered "I will."

    I watch and listen while you tenderly cradle
    my soul with your love, care, respect and

    Support.

Why do you think I have chosen you for my friend?

June 13, 1992

A LETTER WRITTEN BY ME
AS AN ADULT TO MY INNER CHILD

June 13, 1992

Dearest, Sweetest, Gentlest Little Me,

Last night I wrote a poem; I thought I was writing it to my friends. But really, I was writing it from you, little me, to me, the woman and adult. You, little me, thanking me for the care I was taking with our soul.

I remember the first times my therapist tried to explain to me the concept of the inner child within me. I thought that California did not have all the fruits and nuts.

But no more. I have seen you from within. I have heard you tell the stories of the brutality and the power (or powerlessness) under which you lived. I have witnessed the destruction of your being –

That part of you that trusted and loved and respected Dad, so gentle and innocent that could not comprehend the enormity of his betrayal and further the breakdown of the entire family, the destruction of your relationship with Richard, the fear of the anger – the cold, raw, sharp-edged, calculating force that was brought down on you – figuratively and literally. The childlike misunderstanding that if the person who was supposed to protect you and keep you safe could do these things to you, then somehow it must be your fault. And in the acceptance of this came from the forgetting, the desire and drive for perfection, the constant striving to never have anyone annoyed, miffed, mildly put off, and of course never angry. More than that, the desire, almost angelic, to always be poised and in control of yourself lest you cause anyone else, anyone, to become angry and, of course, what I am struggling with now, lest you let out the anger that has built up for so long that I will be so out of control that I will hurt myself, someone else, or go completely crazy.

151

But I will find my anger and you will finally be released from the part of the prison.

How did you survive? I don't mean literally but maybe a better way is to say spiritually. I know the defenses (now) that were mounted by me almost naturally to survive. But spiritually, how did my soul survive? How did I become the me I am now? You are the way and the reason I am me. For this I am eternally grateful to you. You, who suffered so much, made me every day see the suffering of others. You, who was neglected, help me to have a kind word for those who feel neglected. You, who was so traumatized, have helped me protect my own children from the trauma. You, who were never safe, not for one moment after the first attack, have helped me create a safe home for my children. You, who was in so much pain, have helped me to sense pain and react to it instinctively, without thought, to try to ease it in others. You, who never told anyone, have taught me to listen and hear beyond the words. You, who tried always to nurture those around you, have taught me that I have the right to be nurtured myself. You, who was never allowed or free to feel, have taught me to feel. You, who created your own world out of necessity, have taught me to let the rest of the world in. You, who could never be free to share the realities of what was happening to you, have taught me that sharing can be so peaceful and beautiful. How did this spirit survive? I don't know. Why did it survive? It survived so I could become me.

I am not sure that I am ready to say I love, admire, and respect you/me. But maybe that is what this letter is all about. I do know I am ready to accept you and to say I understand, little me, why you had to do some of the things you did to survive. I have truly felt your pain and trauma and witnessed the brutality and reality of your life. I guess I want not to ask, "How did you survive?" But, instead, to say, "Thank you for surviving." We will continue, separately and together, on this path of greater understanding until we can truly become one and find the peace that we deserve.

In closing, little me, thank you for your courage and determination never to give up. It is truly awesome—remarkable beyond words. With you as my model and a part of me, how can I be any less successful in my quest today?

With love, caring, respect, and finally understanding,

Me

MEMORIES OF MY CHILDHOOD

Safe

No place

No one's embrace

Love?

So cold

No one to hold

Anger

Looming

All-consuming

Fear

So near

For many a year

Used

Abused

I got the blues

Looking old

Feeling cold

The terrors unfold

Power!

I cower

As you devour

Gasp

And gape

While you rape

Eyes

So wide

No place to hide

No screams

Or cries

Numb; blank eyes

Behind the

Placid face

A brutal place

I know

I feel

It is revealed

Hope

Not fear

I'm almost there

Peace

So near

But where?

Please come soon!

I need

The answer

To my prayer

June 24, 1992

DON'T YOU UNDERSTAND?

I am worthless

No one wanted me

No one wants me

No one will ever want me

I am nothing

I am garbage

Do what you want with me

How can I get angry with you

      When I am worthless?

I am not worthy of being angry

Why do you think I turn my anger inward?

It is because I don't deserve my own anger;

I don't deserve to direct my anger towards anyone else but me

I am worthless; and, by virtue of that,

I am not allowed to be angry with others

It is but another sign, a reminder, of my worthlessness

My anger was taken away from me so many years ago

In its place, overwhelming worthlessness

Please tell me, write to me, show me, cry with me,

Hold me; I need to know that you understand

July 15, 1992

JOURNALING TO COPE

Anger….it scares me so much. I was consumed by it when I was a child. I was swallowed up by it. It was all around me.

Now, it surrounds me like a haze on a hot, humid day, stifling and oppressive. Frightening like I'm being engulfed in a raging inferno with no escape. Hurting me with the searing pain of burning….burning, burning, burning. My skin is sizzling and crackling; the pain is so intense, so agonizing, so exquisite that I can no longer handle it. So, I pass out. Or I space out and that brings me to the depression.

Depression is what I have become. Now it epitomizes and defines who I am. It is me. I am so over-whelmed by despair, by deep sighs, by the inability to express what is happening to me. I am neither here nor there. I am nowhere. I am in between, in a vacuum, in never-never land. I am floating in a place that has no anchor. I cannot attach myself. Why? Because I am denying my anger.

Please help me. Because if I can learn to accept, to understand, to feel, to embrace, to liberate and to know my anger it will be a giant step in my recovery.

September 19, 1992

September 16, 1994

It seems that lately there is a lot going on in my head. It seems that some significant things have happened of late and they bear reflection and note.

I am at the end of group therapy. It seems like a long journey from a VERY scared person screaming at my therapist that I would never think of going and actually sharing and telling my story to others to someone who feels that I have gotten everything that I can from the group and that it is time to move away. I will very much look forward to having my Tuesday evenings free from now on. It is difficult to believe that I have been a member of the group for two years now.

There is also the issue of moving on in my own personal therapy. I want so much to be able to put all of this in a place that is safe for me. I want to be able to leave it with my therapist and go back to it once a week or so when I want to work on it, not to be carrying it around with me all of the time. I am not exactly sure how to go about this because for me it seems that I need to deal with things when they come up. I'm not sure if this is just my personality or because of what I have been through. Although now that I am more secure the majority of the time that I am safe in the present, maybe I can use that as a way to push off the issues until I am meeting with my therapist. And then, I need to think about these things to some degree to be able to work them through and to understand what is happening and to cope with them. But the key here I guess is not to dwell on this while life is going on, not to let it take over my life.

I must say I have been enjoying living lately. By that I mean that I have been really relishing daily life and the little things that make up any day. I like not waking up in fear and dread and spending the first hour or two each day just trying to get myself to function. I like being able to accomplish things rather than to think, think, think, and to be paralyzed by the night. I am definitely still paralyzed by the night.

I am not yet comfortable with the night. In spite of what has been going on lately I am still having regular nightmares now and that is certainly not pleasant. They are always about my current life. It is as though someone from the past is haunting me and saying that even though I am trying so hard to put the past in the past and I am feeling some success with that, I am now having nightmares about my wonderful present being destroyed. I have one almost every night and usually wake up in a cold sweat feeling very sure that whatever horror has befallen me is absolutely real. I have never had dreams about the present that seemed so real and so terrifying and so uncomfortable. I am experiencing more peace in the present during the day. My concentration is much better, my moods are much better, and I am feeling much better. But I am still haunted in the present during my sleep by thoughts and dreams about things happening in my present. And these thoughts are not truly far-fetched. By that I mean that they are things that could possibly happen, I guess; and they are things that would destroy the happy life that I have now. Like my subconscious is saying that this happy life is just an illusion about to be shattered and that I have no business thinking or feeling otherwise.

About Monday night…it took so much courage to bring my husband with me to see my therapist. It is very complicated for me. I suffered regarding that decision for several days. I had spoken with my therapist on Monday morning and had left it with him so I had a relatively productive day once I got started. When I got home at around 6:30 I started to feel sick. In the car on the way up there I was sure I was going to throw up. The closer I got the worse I felt. And then when I was there I felt sick most of the time. I also spent some of the time tuned out, off in left field somewhere when I felt I couldn't be there anymore.

It was okay. I was okay. Ken was okay. We are supposed to work on me being more comfortable going to bed. Probably for all of these years, going to bed has been uncomfortable for me. Is that a surprise? I guess in a way. I mean I never put a name to it; it was just part of me, part of my normal self. I think a lot of things would be better if I could feel more comfortable about bedtime, being in bed, and sleeping. For me, it felt great and still does not to be alone with all of this. I feel that I have an ally at home now, in a very different way than I felt it before. I remember how it felt when I used to have the panic attacks. At some point I had to tell Ken when they got so bad for me. When I learned to tell him sooner, it helped a lot not to be alone. Maybe this will be the case again. NOT alone.

We are working on me feeling comfortable about the nighttime. I think it is fair to say that I can do this. This does not seem like an insurmountable task. I'm not so sure about the rest yet, but I will work on this part and let the next part come when it comes.

About the past and the present…I know that there will be times when I will feel deeply and horribly the terror and the sadness of what my life was. It was terrible and horrible. I can never change that, no matter what. It can never again be forgotten and it can never be erased and there will never be a time when I won't be sad about my life. But I have a new life now, and it is a good life. That is one of the main reasons why I know it is time to leave group therapy. The other women do not have the great lives that I do. I have a wonderful life. I have a terrific family, many great friends, and my own business that I really enjoy. A perfect life, no. But I do not want or need to be reminded. I will deal with it even though the hurts will still hurt and there will be times when I will need to take time to be hurt. But the pain no longer needs to be the focus of my life.

About the Author

Shirley Aumack was born and lived most of her life in New Jersey along with her husband of 50 years. Together they have two sons and two grandchildren.

In her junior year of high school she was an exchange student to Guatemala. After her marriage, while her husband was in the Air Force, they lived in Italy for three years. Both of  these experiences were life changing. After high school she attended Wilson College in Chambersburg, Pennsylvania, where she majored in Economics and was a DJ and the Station manager of the college radio station.

Her first job was for the New Jersey Bell Telephone Company as the first women hired from outside the company to be in management.

After she had children, she began to work preparing income taxes and eventually started her own business in income tax preparation and financial management which she had for 35 years. During that time she became a Certified Financial Planner and an Enrolled Agent with the Internal Revenue Service in 1987. She became a Collaborative Law Financial Professional in 2009. She taught many seminars and

163

classes over the years including at Rutgers University and many other venues and appeared on national television regarding financial planning for divorce.

During this time she was a licensed life insurance agent and a registered representative with the Securities and Exchange Commission, and she is rightfully most proud that she never had a complaint filed against her by the Financial Industry Regulatory Agency.

She has been in *Who's Who in American Women* since 1993, *Who's Who in Finance and Industry* since 1996 and an *Albert Nelson Marquis Lifetime Achievement Award* recipient since 2019.